PLANET EARTH'S GREATEST MOTORCYCLE ADVENTURE TOURS

PLANET EARTH'S GREATEST MOTORCYCLE ADVENTURE TOURS

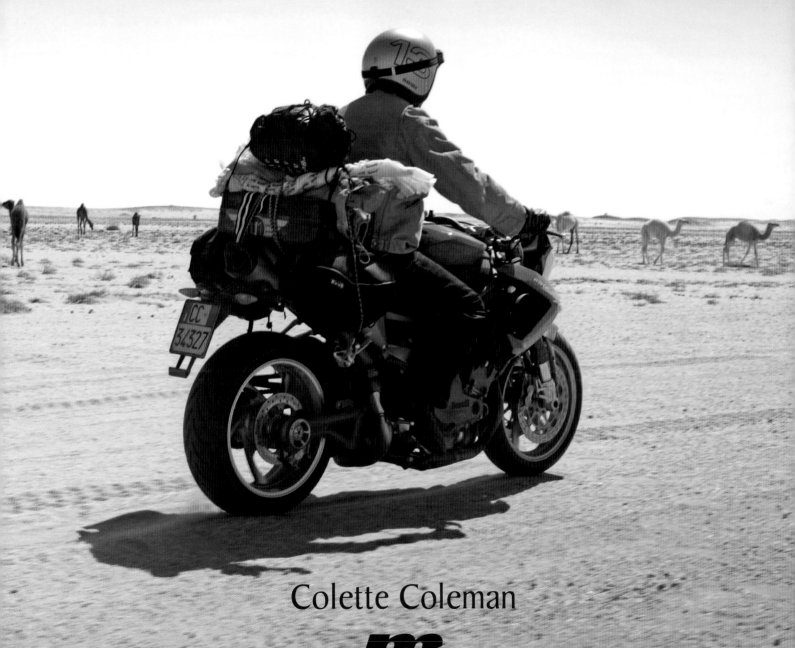

Colette Coleman

m *motorbooks*

This edition published in 2008 by Motorbooks, an imprint of MBI Publishing Company, 400 First Avenue North, Suite 300, Minneapolis, MN 55401 USA

London • Cape Town • Sydney • Auckland
www,newhollandpublishers.com

Motorbooks titles are also available at discounts in bulk quantity for industrial or sales-promotional use. For details write to Special Sales Manager at

MBI Publishing Company, 400 First Avenue North, Suite 300, Minneapolis, MN 55401 USA.
To find out more about our books, join us online at www.motorbooks.com.

ISBN-13: 978-0-7603-3545-1

Library of Congress Cataloging-in-Publication Data

Coleman, Colette.
  Planet earth's greatest motorcycle adventure tours / Colette Coleman.
    p. cm.
  Includes index.
  ISBN 978-0-7603-3545-1 (hb w/ jkt)
  1. Motorcycle touring. 2. Motorcycles. 3. Motorcycles--Pictorial works.
  4. Voyages around the world. I. Title.
  GV1059.5.C59 2008
  796.7'5--dc22
                                    2008019471

Senior Editor: Sarah Goulding
Commissioning EditorL Ross Hilton
Designer: Isabel Gillan
Cartography: Stephen Dew
Picture Research: Joanne Forrest Smith
Production: Marion Storz
Publishing Director: Rpesmary Wilkinson

Reproduction by Pica Digital Pte Ltd, Singapore
Printed and bound by Tien Wah Press Pte Ltd, Singapore

CONTENTS

FOREWORD by Ted Simon

There are so many ways to make discoveries in this world. With a good eye, and in the right frame of mind, even a walk to the office can be an adventure, because journeys, I have always insisted, are made in the imagination. But there is no doubt that the further you go, the more there is for the imagination to feed on.

When I started travelling, as an adolescent immediately after the Second World War, everywhere outside Britain was unknown to me. My first trip, alone by bicycle across an exhausted and war-ravaged France, was as thrilling and demanding as anything I've done since. That wonderful experience lured me back, time and again, to various parts of southern Europe, usually by train or by car, and I became addicted. Like most people I was limited to a few holiday weeks, but I learned how to pack an immense amount into a short time.

Then, in the sixties, I was able for the first time to leave on a journey with no prescribed end in sight. The effect of being able simply to go wherever the wind blew me was quite magical; remarkable opportunities seemed to burst upon me around every corner, and a dazzling sense of liberation made it impossible to go back to a life of office routine. I realized that I was drawn relentlessly to the Mediterranean, and eventually I found a way to live alongside it.

That was just the first time that travel changed my life, but I had still not discovered the motorcycle. Only when I became determined to see the rest of the world did I wake up to the fact that the motorbike really was the perfect vehicle to do this on, and since then I have rarely travelled by any other means. There are so many different degrees of pleasure to be had on a bike; everything from gentle meanderings among the civilized orchards and meadows of Europe, to the wild isolation of the Altiplano in South America. There is something for everyone in the world, just as there is in this book.

Planning a journey can be as much fun as the journey itself. The excitement of trying to picture places and people one has never seen, of trying to anticipate unforeseeable pleasures and problems, of trying to imagine how one will react in a dire situation — these thoughts can make the adrenaline pump. If the journey is a long one through unfamiliar territory — such as

the Silk Road trip described on page 110, for example — it is hard to stop the imagination from working overtime, especially if you expect to ride solo. When I contemplated the journey I had set for myself in 1973, I was sometimes overwhelmed by anxiety about my complete ignorance of the countries and cultures I intended to pass through.

I remember so vividly laying out the three Michelin maps that cover Africa on the living room floor, and being astounded by its vastness. How could I have the temerity to think I would survive all this? But, as someone once said, there are no foreign places, only foreign visitors. I calmed myself by remembering that wherever I went, however exotic it might seem to me, for the people who lived there it was humdrum normality. They survived there from day to day, so why shouldn't I? And once I got going, the immensity of the journey evaporated, and every new day became its own adventure.

Now that I have seen so much, it's easy to forget what a huge rush it can be to wander out into the unknown world, even if what's unknown may lie a relatively short distance away. Anywhere can contain an adventure — even coming back from the Andes and the Himalayas, I was amazed to see just how impressive the European Alps were.

There is so much more to be said, about bikes, equipment, choices (travelling alone or in company), risks and timing, but every rider is different, every journey is unique, and the joy of it is that you can't possibly know what will happen down the road. The important thing is to go, and what better place to start planning your journey than in the pages of this book.

WHY A MOTORCYCLE?

I travel not to go anywhere, but to go. I travel for travel's sake. The great affair is to move.

ROBERT LOUIS STEVENSON

For me, this oft-quoted line sums up completely the joys of travel by motorcycle – whether it is a short ride from home on a crisp, clear morning or a year-long adventure to the other side of the world. The memories that you bring home are of the riding: those days when you and your machine flowed as you wound your way over high passes; or the days when even a few miles seemed to take hours – but the huge sense of achievement as you wearily unpacked your bike at the end of a hard day's ride made you leap out of bed the next day to do it again. It is the riding that you remember the most, the incredible views you saw from the seat of your bike, and the people you met on the journey. Travelling by motorcycle is a wonderful way of meeting people, inspiring interest and passion. Children love them, fellow riders will stop to chat, and for the people you meet on your journey it is a conversation opener – a means of engaging with a complete stranger. Motorcycles are a necessary form of transport in many countries. Many people own one so there is instantly a connection, a shared interest. Motorcycling is also a wonderfully solitary experience, almost a form of mechanical meditation, and yet on your bike you never feel alone.

On a motorcycle you really do feel part of the landscape, completely open to the elements, the noise and the surface of the road. It is only on a bike that you can smell Australian roadkill from a distance of 10 miles, or ride through a busy bazaar and catch the aroma of your lunch before you see it. You can park your motorcycle anywhere – a hotel lobby, or even in your room. If you need to cross countries, vast distances, or find yourself at a closed border, there is always the option to transport your bike by sea, air or train.

Many people dream of travelling by motorcycle, but concerns about their own ability or lack of mechanical knowledge can stop them from taking it any further. You don't have to be an experienced rider or be able to rebuild an engine by the side of the road. You set your own pace and, if there are problems with your bike, you'll always be able to find someone to help. As for dropping your motorcycle – well, if you intend riding on any of

▷ *Off-road biking in South Africa.*

Australia's fantastic dirt roads, the chances are that you probably will. It isn't a big issue. I've yet to own a bike I can pick up, but I've never had a problem finding someone to help. Once you are out there, these issues, if they arise, usually result in new-found friends and a reminder of the kindness of strangers.

The Journeys

The thinking behind this book is that motorcycle travel is so much easier these days, and that any of the featured journeys can be taken as part of an average two- to three-week holiday, a short break taken in your own country, or possibly even a few days out of a family holiday. If you have a little longer, then many of the featured journeys can be linked. It is not necessary to pack up all your possessions, give up your job and take a year out to experience riding in some of the world's most remote regions, but I would definitely recommend it if you can!

▽ *Capital Reef National Park, USA.*

The featured journeys are not a definitive list of the world's best motorcycle trips, but a small selection of journeys that are currently accessible to most nationalities. I have chosen countries where bike hire is available or where there are options to pick up a bike as part of an organized tour. I have included some of the world's classic motorcycle journeys, but also many countries that may not immediately spring to mind when planning a motorcycle trip. I have also tried to include a range of riding terrain. Some countries, such as Morocco, lend themselves to both tarmac and off-road trips. Some routes are considered difficult due to the condition of the roads or the standard of the local driving. There are countries that more naturally lend themselves to relaxed, leisurely riding, combining great roads with sightseeing, good food and accommodation. And then there are routes that really are designed for full-throttle riding. There are also roads that will take you to some of the most beautiful scenery on earth. It is impossible to include all the great riding that some countries offer, but the routes featured provide a flavour of the type of riding you can expect. Many fantastic motorcycle destinations did not make it into the book, either because bike hire or bike-inclusive tours were not available, because the length of the journey was longer than an average holiday, or because current political situations advised avoidance. The Karakorum Highway in Pakistan is an incredible ride, yet a lack of reasonable bike hire and current travel restrictions meant it did not make the final selection. However, these limitations can, and hopefully will, change and open up even more destinations to intrepid motorcyclists.

△ ABOVE LEFT *The lure of the open road can be hard to resist.*

△ ABOVE RIGHT *Travelling with the locals in India.*

Researching this book has been immensely enjoyable, and it has brought back memories of the amazing trips I have taken and the good friends I have made. I have spoken to friends across the globe about their favourite roads and why that journey was so special. I have met operators who started their own tour company purely for the pleasure of meeting other riders and showing them the amazing riding possibilities in their country. The one thing that everyone has in common is their enthusiasm and passion for riding motorcycles.

The Bike

One of the advantages of hiring a bike on arrival is that you get to ride a completely different machine to the bike you have at home. I have occasionally mentioned a particular type of bike when it is so much a part of the experience of the journey. If you've always been a sports-bike rider then perhaps hire a Harley in the USA, or if you have always ridden dual sport bikes, opt for a classic Enfield Bullet in India. The bike you choose can enhance the experience, and may even convert you to a machine you would never otherwise ride. Some countries offer a wide choice of hire bikes, others perhaps only one or two models. Have you ever wondered what it

▽ *Coming face-to-face with Africa's wildlife.*

would be like tackling dirt roads on a Belarusian Minsk 125cc? Try it – you may be pleasantly surprised.

If you plan on taking your own bike, it really isn't necessary to splash out on a new, fully kitted tourer. If you are comfortable with your current bike, then always consider taking it. A motorcycle will go anywhere; some are just better suited to challenging terrain than others. There is an amazing choice of great motorcycles and the decision is generally down to your budget or favoured brand. Look at your chosen route, comfort and luggage-carrying capacity. The bike's off-road ability and fuel range may also have a bearing. There are no hard and fast rules. All types of motorcycle can be, and have been, used for journeys across the globe.

Travel Requirements

The internet has made planning a motorcycle trip so much easier. It is now possible to arrange bike hire, book organized trips, or arrange the freight of your own machine with the click of a computer mouse. You can read about other people's journeys and email questions to riders on the other side of the globe. This book does not go into any detail regarding visas, *carnets de passage* or health checks, as these all differ depending on nationality, and can change regularly and without warning. The contacts listed on pages 190–91 will help you get started, but then it is up to you. Half the fun of any motorcycle trip is in the excitement of planning the route, deciding the type of riding you want to experience and choosing the bike. Ultimately everyone's trip is unique, and the final decision regarding route and motorcycle will be yours.

△ *If you choose to travel alone, you can be sure of meeting like-minded friends along the way.*

Final Words

As you load up your bike, the anticipation of the adventures in store, the challenge of the riding ahead, and the knowledge that you and your motorcycle can go anywhere is a feeling that only motorcyclists can describe. Setting out on any motorcycle journey is supremely exciting and I hope that the following journeys will inspire you to break out and explore the world on, without doubt, the very best form of motorized transport – the motorcycle.

OVERLEAF *Dune riding in spectacular scenery.*

AFRICA

Ceuta to Marrakech Loop

Ride over the Atlas Mountains, across the deserts of the Sahara and alongside the wild Atlantic coast.

Mysterious Morocco is so close to Europe, yet seems a world and several centuries away. The colourful bazaars of the imperial cities, the deserts of the Sahara, and the lush palm-filled oases all provide a tantalizing taste of North Africa. There are accommodation options for every budget, from desert campsites to luxurious *riads* (traditional Moroccan dwellings with interior gardens). The sheer diversity of the landscape and culture is hard to beat, making a visit to Morocco a wonderfully varied and rewarding experience.

▽ *The Tizi n'Test Pass in the High Atlas Mountains.*

Morocco is a fantastic winter escape for motorcyclists, offering an exciting range of riding possibilities. Time and ability really isn't an issue as there is just so much choice. Two of the best road-riding routes in Morocco take you over the high passes of the Tizi n'Tichka and the Tizi n'Test, and both connect the desert towns of the south to the imperial city of Marrakesh. For off-road riders there are mule tracks, dry riverbeds, deep sand and plenty of *fesh fesh* (bull dust, or sand as fine as talcum powder). Trails are endless, with Morocco often forming part of the world-famous Paris–Dakar Rally. Fuel is easily available throughout the country, but check in advance where your next fuel stop is located if you head off-road or into the desert.

The Route

Allow roughly two weeks for the following route, which combines great road riding with city sightseeing, desert and mountain scenery, and wild Atlantic beaches.

Roll off the ferry at Spanish-owned Ceuta, entering Morocco at the northern tip. Head south for 100 km (62 miles) through the wild and isolated Rif Mountains to Chefchaouen, a picturesque town of narrow streets and white-washed houses nestling between two mountains. Enjoy the relaxed atmosphere for a few days, then head south to Fez. The little-used but absolutely awesome switchbacks of the Route de L'Unite, via Ketama, wind for over 270 km (168 miles) through the wild, lawless heart of the mountainous Rif region, where *kif* (marijuana) covers the surrounding hills and is the main economy of the region. The *medina* (literally 'city', now used for the original Arab part of any Moroccan town) in Fez is one of the largest in the world. Thousands of craftsmen work in a warren of *souks*, or bazaars, their tiny shops spilling out onto noisy, pungent alleyways that lead to palaces, mosques and *medersas* (student residences). Leave your bike (and those heavy boots!) at the hotel and lose yourself in Morocco's oldest imperial city.

Sahara-bound, the 435 km (270 mile) ride south to Erfoud crosses the Middle and High Atlas Mountains. The traffic is light and road surfaces generally good, making the ride enjoyable and reasonably fast. Once over the Atlas at Er Rachida, the plains and palmeries start to melt into the Sahara proper. From Erfoud, ride out to the Erg Chebbi sand dunes and perfect your sand-riding techniques, or exchange your motorcycle for a camel and head into the desert for a few days. Once you've finished playing in the sand, take the road west for around 125 km (78 miles) to the magnificent gorges of Todra and Boumalne du Dades. Road bikes will have no problem negotiating the 25 km (16 mile) paved road at either entrance, and riders on a dual sport bike can follow the well-maintained tracks that

△ *A bustling souk in Marrakesh, Morocco.*

connect the two. There are a number of small hotels within the gorges, so stay overnight and watch the setting sun turn the gorges crimson whilst sipping 'whiskey berber'.

From Boumalne du Dades, head 135 km (84 miles) west to Ouarzazate, the largest town in the south and the start of a ride to Marrakech via the fabulous Tizi n'Tichka Pass. The winding but well paved 170 km (106 mile) road is lined with Berber villages and crumbling *kasbahs* (citadels). It can easily be ridden in a day but there are numerous opportunities to detour from the main road. About an hour north of Ouarzazate, a 20 km (12 mile) road runs off to the *kasbah* of Ait Benhaddou, one of the locations for the filming of *Lawrence of Arabia* and, more recently, *Gladiator*. An overnight stop in the nearby village ensures fabulous views of the *kasbah* over breakfast.

Rejoining the main road, watch out for the turn-off to a bumpy track about 50 km (31 miles) further north. The 44 km (27 mile) track takes you to the crumbling *kasbah* of Telouet, set against a backdrop of stark mountains that turn almost black in the changing

BIKE: It is possible to take your own bike into Morocco. Bike hire is limited, but there are operators offering bike-inclusive tours.

WEATHER WATCH: Morocco is a year-round destination. However, June to September is very hot, especially in the desert. Expect snow in the mountains from November to February.

EXTENDING THE RIDE: A short ferry ride from Tangier or Ceuta (Spain) will take you to Andalucia in southern Spain.

light. If you've got a dual sport bike, there is a challenging track connecting these two *kasbahs*. Return to the main road for the final 110 km (68 miles) to Marrakech. Be warned, though, that negotiating the labyrinthine alleys of the old city can be hair-raising. Spend a few days soaking up the atmosphere of this medieval city that seems unchanged by the centuries and watch in amusement as acrobats, storytellers and snake charmers skilfully extract *dirhams* from visitors and locals alike on the Djema El Fna. However, if you just can't get enough of the twisting, mountainous roads, then load up the bike and head south again to the fabulous Tizi n'Test Pass. The road is remote and cuts through the heart of the Atlas mountains linking Marrakech with the Souss plain and the deserts beyond. Hairpin bends and spectacular views abound for over 220 km (137 miles) to Taroudant in the Souss Valley. From Taroudant, head west for an hour to the coast. The route north to Ceuta hugs the Atlantic, following well-maintained roads, including a section of motorway. There are numerous towns and villages along the coast, and the white-washed town of Essaouira, a 260 km (162 mile) ride from Taroudant, is a relaxing place to spend a few days, before continuing for a further 400 km (249 miles) up the coast to Rabat. A mix of French-styled boulevards and historical Arab monuments, Rabat feels surprisingly sleepy for a capital city. From here a 320 km (199 mile) ride north takes you to back to Ceuta, leaving a country that should have you already planning your next trip as the ferry heads back across the Straits of Gibraltar.

△ *Boumalne du Dades at dusk.*

▽ *Morocco is an ideal winter escape.*

Nairobi to the Central Highlands and the Great Rift Valley

From Nairobi ride to the lush Central Highlands and the jagged snow-capped peaks of Mount Kenya, crossing the Equator on stunning roads that link the lakes and canyons of the Great Rift Valley.

The Central Highlands and Great Rift Valley provide an amazing variety of landscapes and wildlife. Tropical jungle and lush plantations give way to forested escarpments and spectacular valleys, revealing vast lakes teeming with birdlife. The beautiful acacia forests of Nakuru National Park – made famous in the film *Out of Africa* – boast an incredible variety of wildlife. Kenya's impressive accommodation is all part of the experience, and a wonderful treat after a long day's ride. Kick off your boots and relax in style at luxurious lodges and tented camps, affording stunning views of waterholes or mountain peaks.

Good tarmac gives way to bumpy, potholed roads then reappears again for long stretches. Unlike some parts of Africa, where roads quickly become impassable with a little rain, the main road surfaces of northern Kenya are generally good. This is a motorcycle ride in Africa that will take you to mountains, valleys and game parks along roads that, whilst not perfect, do not require off-road skills, a fully loaded dual sport and a week's supply of fuel. The riding is fun and not too hurried, as you travel along roads dug from a rich, red volcanic earth that contrast beautifully with the surrounding lush, green vegetation.

The Route

This route takes you through the Central Highlands and across the Great Rift and should take a week to ten days, allowing time to combine your riding with game drives and highland walks.

Ride out of Nairobi heading for Mount Kenya about 245 km (152 miles) northeast. The area is extensively farmed and Kenya's excellent coffee is cultivated in this rich, volcanic soil. As you ride, Mount Kenya is visible in the distance, its twin peaks often shrouded in cloud. It is a stunningly beautiful mountain, and at 5,199 m (17,058 ft) is Africa's second highest peak. Stay around the town of Naru Moro for fabulous views, and hire guides for the trek to the peak or take a wonderful day-walk up the lower slopes, passing through luxuriant, tropical vegetation.

▷ *The stunning Great Rift Valley in Africa.*

△ *Flamingos at Lake Bogoria, Kenya.*

▽ *The official Equator line in Nanyuki, Kenya.*

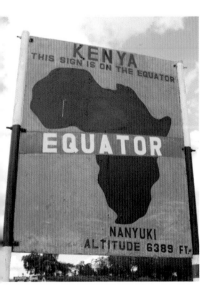

From Naru Moru continue north for about an hour to the Equator sign at Nanyuki, which has got to be worth a photograph sat astride your motorcycle. Skirt the Equator for around 100 km (62 miles) along a largely unsurfaced road to Nyahururu – at 2,360 m (7,743 ft) Kenya's highest town – then drop southwest descending into the Great Rift Valley, arriving at Nakuru National Park before sunset. In addition to its famous flamingo population, Nakuru is also a great place to see black and white rhino, and leopard sightings are frequent. Park your bike up for a couple of days and take advantage of the game drives offered by the lodges and campsites in and around the park.

Temperatures rise dramatically and the vegetation becomes sparser as you ride the 60 km (37 miles) north from Nakuru to Lake Bogoria, a soda lake of boiling-hot springs, geysers and steam jets. Thousands of flamingos and birds inhabit a lake surrounded by a barren and rocky landscape, evidence of the volcanic origins of the Rift Valley. In stark contrast, the freshwater Lake Baringo, less than an hour's ride north, is a lush, green oasis. Unpack the panniers and spend a few days relaxing beside the lake and exploring the area on two wheels minus your luggage. Join an early morning boat trip to see fish eagles, crocodiles and hippos, then take a fantastic 273 km (170 mile) loop over the Tugen Hills into the Kerio Valley. From the town of Marigat, central to both lakes, ride a paved road that climbs and winds through magnificent scenery to Kabarnet in the Tugen Hills, before plunging from the Elgeyo Escarpment into the beautiful Kerio Valley. Views are fabulous as the road snakes across canyons and ridges. Return to Lake Baringo for a sundowner whilst watching the hippos leave the water to graze.

◁ *Meeting the local Maasai in Kenya.*

OVERLEAF *African sunset.*

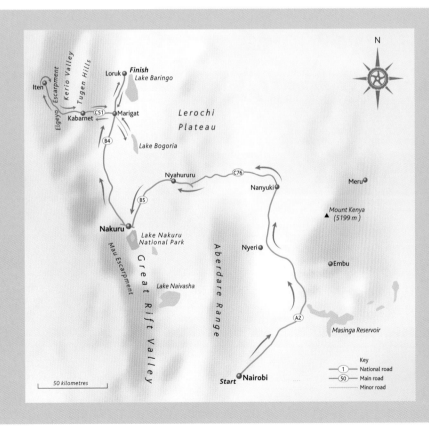

tool box

BIKE: It is possible to take your own bike into Kenya. Bike hire is available in Nairobi. There are operators offering bike-inclusive tours.

WEATHER WATCH: December to mid-March is the best time to visit, although there can be light rains in December. The wettest period is during April and May.

EXTENDING THE RIDE: No overland connection to other featured journeys.

Windhoek to Etosha National Park

This route ventures south from Windhoek to the sand dunes of the Namib Desert before heading north through the remote, arid wilderness and desolate mountain scenery of Damaraland to Etosha National Park.

Namibia is a country of contrasts and one of Africa's best kept secrets. Ride past table-topped mountains, through lunar landscapes and across vast open plains enjoying an exhilarating sense of space and freedom. Discover the colossal sand dunes of the world's oldest desert, and exquisite rock art that has survived for thousands of years in cool canyons, away from the scorching heat. Meet the statuesque and beautiful tribal people that populate this ancient land, but best of all experience the unforgettable sight of rare desert elephants and black rhino crossing the road ahead of you as they roam freely across this vast, beautiful land.

▽ *Expect to see stunning desert scenery in Namibia.*

A network of well-maintained, graded gravel roads criss-cross the country – about 70 per cent of Namibia's roads are unsealed. It is not difficult to ride on the loose mix of sand and gravel, but you need to keep your wits about you. Negotiate dry riverbeds, cross patches of sand and ride all day on empty roads that stretch as far as the eye can see. The heat haze sits on the horizon as you weave through vast expanses of arid wilderness, leaving a trail of dust in your wake. There are lodges and tented camps, but pack your tent as well – this is a motorcycle journey that lends itself to days of solitary riding and nights spent under thousands of stars beside a glowing camp fire.

△ The view from the footpegs is frequently breathtaking.

The Route

A week to ten days will give you time to combine riding with a visit to some of Namibia's top sights.

Head straight for the Namib Desert around 402 km (250 miles) southwest of Windhoek. The gravel road climbs the Kupferberg Pass followed by fantastic views from the Spreetshoogte Pass before descending into the Namib Desert at Sesriem, gateway to the world's highest dunes. Camp under the shade of acacia trees and gaze at the night stars, rising early to watch the sunrise over the dunes.

Enjoy the cool desert air as you ride into the Tsauchab Valley on a road that is paved for 60 km (27 miles), followed by 5 km (3 miles) through heavy sand to the dunes at Sossusvlei. There is a shuttle service if you don't want to ride this final tricky section. The mountainous dunes are an awesome 300 m (985 ft) high, and dwarf everything in sight. Sculpted by the wind, the shifting sands are constantly changing shape, whilst the movement of the hot desert sun changes their colour throughout the day, culminating in a fiery display at sunset.

From Sesriem head north on gravel roads for around 300 km (186 miles) via the Gaub Pass and the spectacular, barren landscape of Kuiseb Canyon. Join a paved road for the short final section from Walvis Bay to Swakopmund, a charming coastal town and a centre for activity-based sports. The nearby dunes provide the opportunity to spend a day quad-biking or dune-boarding.

From Swakopmund the road follows the coast north for around 75 km (47 miles) to Henties Bay, where you head inland riding deep into the dry desert landscape of Damaraland along long stretches of road and across dry riverbeds. In the Twyfelfontein area, follow dusty tracks to ancient bushman rock art and a petrified forest over 200 million years

▽ BELOW LEFT *The mountain scenery in Namibia makes for an unforgettable trip.*

▽ BELOW RIGHT *Dune riding is easier on quad-bikes than by motorcycle.*

old. End your long day's ride below Brandberg Mountain as it glows in the setting sun, before making camp nearby on the banks of the Aba-Huab River and enjoying a campfire supper under wide African skies.

Rising early next morning, ride into the vast plains of northern Damaraland, scouring the landscape as you ride in search of the elusive desert elephants. Comfortable tented camps scatter this remote region, many offering guided wildlife tours.

Refuel at Palmweg then ride up and over the Grootberg Pass, heading east for around 250 km (155 miles) to join the C38, which leads to the main entrance of Etosha National Park. Wash off the dust and relax at comfortable lodges, taking guided drives into the park to observe the rare and endangered wildlife that roam one of the greatest game parks in southern Africa.

BIKE: It is possible to take your own bike into Namibia. Bike hire is available in Windhoek. There are operators offering bike-inclusive tours.

WEATHER WATCH: May to September is the best time to visit. November to March is the wettest period.

EXTENDING THE RIDE: Link up to a trip in neighbouring South Africa. It is around 1,500 km (932 miles) from Windhoek to Cape Town, or a two-hour flight.

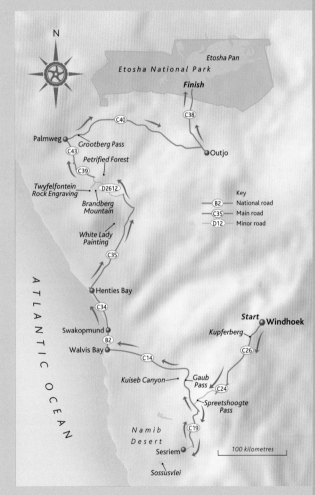

Cape Town Circuit through the Garden Route

A circular ride of the Western and Eastern Capes that encompasses South Africa's coast, plains and winelands.

▽ *Cape Point, where the Atlantic and Indian Oceans meet.*

Beautiful, cosmopolitan Cape Town nestles in the shadow of Table Mountain, an inviting and relaxed city and the perfect starting point for a ride through the Western and Eastern Cape. Roads weave through the tranquil valleys of the Winelands, follow the coastal Garden Route past forested mountains and white-sand beaches, before heading inland to the endless skies and vast plains of the Karoo. The region offers accommodation to suit all tastes and budgets, an incredible variety of seafood and, of course, South Africa's award-winning wines.

South Africa has long been a favourite motorcycle destination. Its wide choice of bike hire and fabulous roads make it an easy and enjoyable fly-ride holiday. The Western and Eastern Capes have great tarmac roads that wind through stunning scenery and a Mediterranean climate that all motorcyclists love. There are also plenty of opportunities to get off-road and put that hired dual sport bike to the test.

The Route

Allowing for sightseeing and time off the bike, this is roughly a two-week circuit that sticks to the tarmac but with options to get on the dirt.

Leaving Cape Town, the fun begins just east of Hout Bay along Chapman's Peak Drive, 10 km (6 miles) of thrilling, twisting riding along a cliff-edge road that boasts an incredible 114 bends, with the wild Atlantic Ocean swirling below. The road leads to the Cape of Good Hope, where the Atlantic and Indian Oceans smash into each other at Cape Point. Dismount for a few moments to absorb the fantastic views of the crashing surf and the dramatic windswept coastline. Leave the Cape via False Bay, following the coast road from the Strand to Hermanus, which lies around 115 km (71 miles) east of Cape Town and is famed for its seafood and visiting whales. An enjoyable 150 km (93 miles) of sweeping bends lead slightly inland before dropping south to Cape Agulhas, the southernmost point of Africa. Spend the night here or further down the coast at the pretty village of Arniston.

A 250 km (155 mile) ride northeast on the N2 takes you to Mossel Bay, the start of the famous Garden Route, which runs for 185 km (115 miles) to Storms River Mouth. The road winds through tranquil countryside, below rocky cliffs and alongside wild, sandy beaches. It can easily be ridden in a few hours, but with a wide choice of hotels and restaurants scattered along the route it is worth a few day's leisurely ride. Adrenaline junkies can abseil, bungee jump and even swim with sharks. About halfway along, the pretty town of Knysna makes a good overnight stop. The town is surrounded by a beautiful lagoon which empties into the Indian Ocean at the dramatic cliffs known as The Heads. Overnight here and dine on the town's speciality – delicious fresh oysters.

Heading into the Eastern Cape, leave the N2 briefly and detour onto the old road for a scenic, twisting ride over the Grootrivier and Bloukrans Passes, then drop down to Storms River Mouth and Tsitsikamma National Park, an area of rocky coast and indigenous ancient forest, with a marine reserve that stretches over 5 km (3 miles) out to sea. Port Elizabeth, a further 200 km (124 miles) east, is where you leave the coast behind and head inland for around 300 km (186 miles) towards the Karoo Nature Reserve and the semi-desert of the

▽ *Riding the sand dunes in South Africa.*

African bush. A ride north over the Olifantskop Pass leads you to the turn-off for Addo National Park and the chance to see big game.

Returning to the main road, continue north crossing the Sneeuberg Mountain via Wapadsberg and Nauderberg Passes before descending to the historic town of Graaff-Reinet in the heartland of the Great Karoo. Just out of town, ride along a narrow, paved road that climbs the mountains for stunning sunset views down to the Valley of Desolation. Stay in the area and experience life on a sheep farm at one of the traditional farmstays.

Vast horizons surround you as you ride a fast 300 km (186 miles) through flat plains to Oudtshoorn, the principle town of Little Karoo. Base yourself in the area for a few days and take advantage of the great riding on offer. Oudtshoorn grew rich from the Victorian fashion for large feathers, and for the lighter-framed motorcyclist there is the chance to visit a farm and take an ostrich ride. If that doesn't get the adrenaline going, then take a ride into Hell. Gamkaskloof, commonly known as Die Hel or 'The Hell', is an awesome dirt road

BIKE: It is possible to take your own bike into South Africa. Bike hire is available in Cape Town. There are operators offering bike-inclusive tours.

WEATHER WATCH: March and April or September and October are the best times to visit. The wettest period is from May to August.

EXTENDING THE RIDE: Link up to a trip in neighbouring Namibia. It is around 1,500 km (932 miles) from Cape Town to Windhoek, or a two-hour flight.

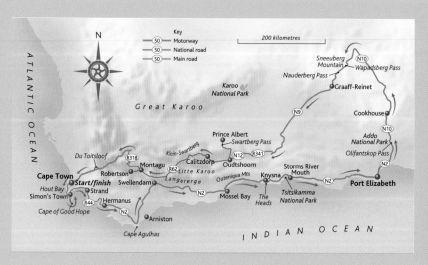

that leads to a dramatic valley forming part of the Swartberg Nature Reserve. It is reached from the summit of the Swartberg Pass, which lies between Oudtshoorn and the town of Prince Albert, 70 km (43 miles) north. If you want to spend the night in Hell, there are camping facilities in the valley. Alternatively, take a ride over the unpaved mountain hairpins of the Swartberg Pass, returning to Oudtshoorn via the paved Meiringspoort Pass, which crosses the Groot River 26 times. The mountains and valleys of Little Karoo are connected by a series of fantastic passes that twist, climb and switchback through a wild, rugged landscape. Leave Oudtshoorn heading west on Route 62 and you get to ride them all. A 220 km (137 mile) ride brings you to the town of Robertson, one of the many lovely towns of the Winelands, which lie just a few hours east of Cape Town. Stay at one of the traditional farmsteads, enjoy local food and wine, and take a ride out to the historic estates and vineyards that nestle below towering mountains.

△ *Riding through 'Hell'.*

◁ *If you are lucky, encounters with wildlife will be part of your African adventure.*

OVERLEAF *Stopping to admire the view in the Torres del Paine National Park, Chile.*

THE AMERICAS

Anchorage to Whitehorse Loop

Ride a great figure-of-eight loop through the wilds of the northeastern part of the North American continent.

It can be difficult to comprehend the sheer size and sparseness of population when first looking at a map of this area. Huge mountain ranges and snow-capped peaks are often visible as you ride along highways stretching off into the distance. The Yukon Territory is a vast area of forests, lakes, rivers and rolling hills. The St Elias Mountains run through the southwest corner and contain Canada's highest peak, Mount Logan. In the west lie the famous Yukon and Klondike rivers, scene of North America's last great gold rush. Alaska consists of a giant plateau containing many long mountain ranges, which you will often ride alongside. In the centre is Denali National Park. There are only two settlements of any size, Anchorage and Fairbanks; everything else is small by comparison, although good camping and inexpensive hostels can be found along the route.

The area is not always in the grip of a deep-freeze and the riding conditions in summer can be excellent – but don't forget your waterproof gear, as rain is not uncommon. Mosquito repellent is also a must. Wildlife is abundant here and it is quite possible to see moose and bears by the road – just don't let them get too close! The road surfaces on this route are mostly excellent and nearly all sealed. You can hit the dirt on side trips if you wish, but a road bike will be perfectly adequate. Because of the mountainous terrain there are plenty of twisting parts interspersed with long, fast straights, so lengthy distances can be covered quickly.

The Route

This route will give a great taste of the semi-tamed wilderness in this part of the world. It can be ridden in two to three weeks, with stops at places of interest or even a short walk in one of the national parks if you fancy a break from sitting on a bike.

The start of the trip is Alaska's capital, Anchorage. Head north on the state's only multi-lane freeway, which you soon leave behind, and join the George Parks Highway with the spectacular Chugach Mountains to your right. After 161 km (100 miles) of riding,

▽ *Be sure to pack your cold weather gear when riding in Alaska.*

you'll reach the turn-off to the town of Talkeetna. This is the base for flights over the Denali Range, and it is well worth breaking your journey to take a flight over the giant glaciers and peaks. Denali National Park is to your left as you continue north over the 701 m (2,300 ft) high Broad Pass to the park turn-off. Access is by shuttle bus only, but is well worth a visit if you have the time. It is 579 km (360 miles) from Anchorage to Fairbanks, and the last section winds through the Tanana Hills, offering great riding with good views of the Alaska Range to the east. It is also one of the few places in Alaska where you can legally ride at 65 mph (105 kph)!

▽ *The tranquil scenery of the Denali National Park, Alaska.*

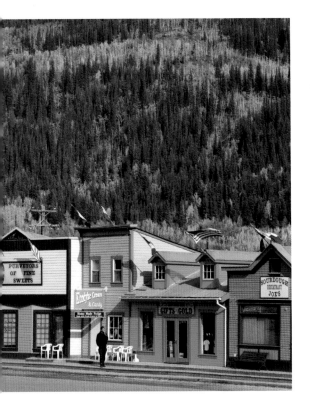

Fairbanks is only a quarter of the size of Anchorage and certainly feels like a town on the edge of things. It can reach -51°C (-60°F) in winter and 38°C (100°F) in summer, one of the biggest city temperature ranges in the world. Relax after a few long days in the saddle in one of the hot springs around town. It is here that you can turn north for a 1,448 km (900 mile) return side trip up the Dalton Highway or Haul Road, crossing the Arctic Circle and ending in Deadhorse. The road is unsealed and follows the Alaskan oil pipeline, crossing some of the most spectacular and wild terrain accessible in the state.

Leave Fairbanks and head southeast on the Alaska Highway through the great interior plateau. It is 322 km (200 miles) to Tok with only the small town of Delta Junction in between, so it can seem pretty lonely out there. Shortly after you reach Tetlin Junction, head off left onto what is called the Klondike Loop. This consists of the Taylor Highway (Alaska), Klondike and Top of the World Highways (Canada) and ends in Whitehorse in the Yukon Territory. The first section of the loop takes you through the town of Chicken, into the Yukon and on to Dawson City. The Top of the World Highway is 322 km (200 miles) of wide, smooth dirt climbing over

BIKE: It is possible to take your own bike into Canada and Alaska. You can hire bikes in Anchorage. There are operators offering bike-inclusive tours.

WEATHER WATCH: Mid-May to mid-September is really the only time to ride this route by motorcycle.

EXTENDING THE RIDE: Link this trip with a ride in the Canadian Rockies. Calgary is 3,438 km (2,130 miles) from Anchorage and 2,293 km (1,425 miles) from Whitehorse.

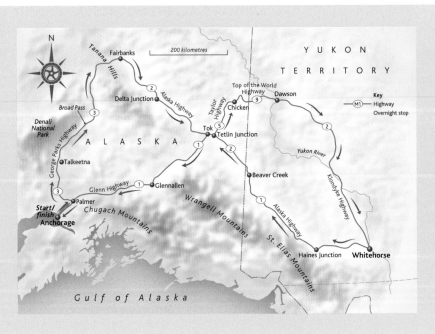

the alpine tundra, with fantastic views of the road running along ridge tops into the distance before you take the ferry over the Yukon River into town. Dawson City is a fascinating place and one of the highlights of the trip. It was the centre of the Klondike Gold Rush, and many old buildings have been restored. You can pan for gold and visit the largest wooden-hulled gold dredge in North America, built in 1912. From here it is 500 km (311 miles) to Whitehorse on the banks of the Yukon River, the largest city in northern Canada. It also has its share of gold rush history, and a large restored paddle steamer is berthed at the end of town.

Leaving Whitehorse, you head 805 km (500 miles) northwest back on the Alaska Highway. After riding through the small settlement of Haines Junction, the Kluane Icefield Ranges and St Elias Mountains dominate the view to your left as you cruise along the perfect, sealed highway and, shortly after the town of Beaver Creek, you cross back over the border into Alaska headed back to Tok. From here, it's time to complete the large figure-of-eight loop back to Anchorage along the Glenn Highway, a distance of 531 km (330 miles). Head towards Glennallen along a beautiful stretch of road, with the Wrangell Mountains to your left. From Glennallen the highway winds over the 914 m (3,000 ft) Tahnita Pass. This section is wonderfully scenic, especially in August when many trees turn gold and have a backdrop of snowy peaks and glaciers. You are on the last leg of your journey now through the town of Palmer to join the freeway back into Anchorage, after your epic ride through the wilderness.

◁ *Dawson City was at the heart of the gold rush in the early 20th century.*

▽ *The St Elias Mountains make a stunning backdrop.*

The Rockies: Calgary to Jasper

*This route runs from Calgary to Jasper National Park,
through the heart of the Canadian Rockies.*

▽ Riding in the Rockies.

The Canadian Rockies run through the provinces of Alberta and British Columbia in western Canada, spanning almost 1,500 km (932 miles) as far as the Yukon border. Soaring peaks tower over a pristine, unspoilt wilderness of forest, glacial lakes, canyons and valleys. The sheer immensity and beauty of the landscape is hard to imagine and the scenery that unfolds before you will surpass all expectations.

There is a short summer season for a motorcycle trip in the Rockies, when the snow has finally melted and it is warm enough to hit the road on a bike. This is a ride through Canada's big outdoors and the weather can quickly change, so pack plenty of layers and keep them to hand. The main road surfaces are excellent, giving you time to admire breathtaking views from the saddle. Snow-capped peaks appear around every bend and there are regular viewpoints along the way for you to pull over and admire the scenery. The ride along the Icefields Parkway is absolutely spectacular, and has to rate as one of the world's classic motorcycle rides.

△ *The stunning views at Peyto Lake should not be missed.*

The Route

A week will allow time for exploring the national parks in between riding this 450 km (280 mile) route.

The city of Calgary nestles between the Rockies and the rolling prairies and provides the perfect springboard for a ride into the Rockies themselves. It is a fast and pleasant 130 km (81 mile) ride on the Trans-Canada Highway to Banff National Park. The resort of Banff is a lively town and the main base for exploring the wooded valleys, peaks and crystal waters of possibly the most famous park of the Canadian Rockies.

▷ *The Icefields Parkway cuts through the Rockies and offers spectacular views.*

From Banff, take the scenic Bow Valley Parkway to Lake Louise. It is a short ride at just over 55 km (34 miles), but the views are magnificent, so slow down the pace, relax into the ride and enjoy the scenery. The village of Lake Louise is located in the Bow Valley and provides accommodation and information. The lake itself lies just 4 km (2.5 miles) above the village along the winding Lake Louise Drive. Turquoise blue and dominated by the Victoria Glacier, it is a truly breathtaking sight, its perfection seeming almost unreal. An enjoyable, winding 13 km (8 mile) ride leads to the smaller but possibly even more beautiful Moraine Lake, its waters surrounded by ten glaciated summits.

Returning to Lake Louise, head north to Jasper National Park along the Icefields Parkway, which cuts through the heart of the Rockies and crosses through both Banff and Jasper National Parks. Ride the 230 km (143 miles) in a day or pull over for a few nights on the way and explore the region. There are campsites, youth hostels and a few hotels along the route. Described by early fur traders as the 'Wonder Trail', the unending succession of gorgeous turquoise lakes, vast walls of ice and row after row of jagged peaks provide

▽ *A glacier in the Columbia Icefields in the Rockies.*

unforgettable views for most of the ride. The road climbs steadily for 40 km (25 miles) through a sub-alpine forest up to Bow Summit, which at 2,068 m (6,785 ft) is the highest point on the Parkway. The fantastic views at the nearby Peyto Lake viewpoint should not be missed.

The road then starts to drop for the following 37 km (23 miles) to Saskatchewan Crossing, where you can top up with fuel before the steep climb towards the Columbia Icefields, the largest collection of ice and snow in the Rockies. You can take a Snocoach tour or even an ice-walk right out onto the Athabasca Glacier. From here the road begins a gradual descent towards the sleepy town of Jasper, at the end of the Parkway. Roll into town and enjoy its laid-back atmosphere while you explore the huge, rugged wilderness of Jasper National Park..

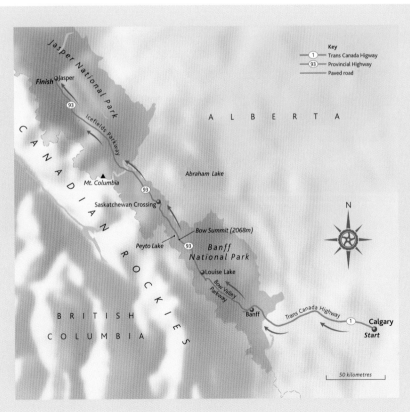

tool box

BIKE: It is possible to take your own bike into Canada. Bike hire is available in Calgary or Vancouver. There are operators offering bike-inclusive tours.

WEATHER WATCH: June to September is really the only time to ride this route by motorcycle.

EXTENDING THE RIDE: Link this trip with a ride in the Yukon and North West Territories. Anchorage is 3,438 km (2,130 miles) from Calgary and Whitehorse is 2,293 km (1,425 miles).

Montreal to the Gaspé Peninsula

*Ride from Montreal following the north shore of the St Lawrence River
to Baie Comeau, crossing to the scenic roads of the Gaspé Peninsula.*

▽ *The busy skyline of
Quebec City.*

French-speaking Quebec is totally unique within North America. A province of contrasts, it blends old world and new, featuring stylish cities within an awe-inspiring wilderness. Stretching almost 2,000 km (1,243 miles) from north to south, the northern regions encompass enormous expanses of forest and tundra. Southern Quebec is easily accessible and split by the St Lawrence River, which flows from the Great Lakes to the Atlantic Ocean.

On this route you can dine on fine, French cuisine and ride the Chemin du Roy, or 'Royal Way'. Follow the St Lawrence River on winding roads and through pretty villages along La Route des Baleines, or 'the Whale Route', then cross to the Gaspé Peninsula, which juts into the ocean for over 500 km (310 miles). This is a motorcycle ride that takes you through a land of mountains, vast lakes and mighty rivers, and with a good range of accommodation options and the choice of riding short daily distances, it is a journey that can be done at a leisurely pace.

The Route

The following route gives you a taste of the southeast region of this huge country. Ten days to two weeks will allow for time off the bike to explore the national parks.

From Montreal, motor along the Chemin du Roy. This route was built in 1735 to link Montreal, Trois Rivières and Quebec City, and for over a century conveyed mail and

▽ *Parked up to take a break in Montreal.*

travellers by stagecoach or sleigh, via 29 relay stations. At full gallop the journey could be made in two days. Today it is an easy day's ride, as HW138 follows the old road for approximately 250 km (155 miles), meandering through beautiful scenery and picturesque villages along the north shore of the mighty St Lawrence River towards Quebec City, a capital that combines its modern French style with ancient cobbled streets and historic buildings.

From Quebec City, La Route des Baleines runs for 266 km (165 miles) to Baie Comeau, where you cross to the Gaspé Peninsula. Running through the beautiful UNESCO-protected Charlevoix region, which stretches from the Beaupre Coast to the Saguenay Fjord, the road winds through rural villages, valleys and rolling hills. At the pretty town of Baie St Paul take the coast-hugging HW362, which twists and turns through many hilltop villages.

BIKE: It is possible to take your own bike into Canada. Bike hire is available in Montreal. There are operators offering bike-inclusive tours.

WEATHER WATCH: Mid-May to mid-October is the best time to visit.

EXTENDING THE RIDE: Head from Montreal to Vermont for a ride around New England, or from the Gaspé Peninsula ride through New Brunswick to Nova Scotia.

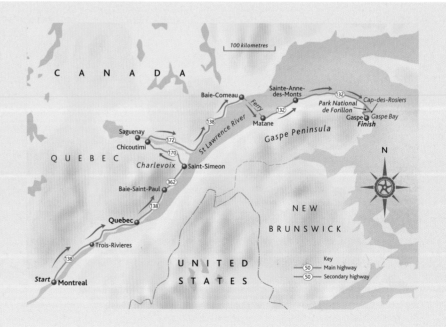

The soft landscape eventually gives way to more dramatic rocky outcrops and sheer cliffs, where the Saguenay River meets one of the world's longest fjords and smashes its way into the St Lawrence River. This mixing of the cold sea waters with the freshwater of the Saguenay River produces a rich crop of plankton, and in the summer months migratory whales flock to the area to feed. To see so many species of whale in one area is a magical and humbling experience.

From Saint-Siméon the HW170 twists its way for 125 km (78 miles) to the Parc du Saguenay, hitting the enormous fjord after about 50 km (31 miles). There are no bridges until the crossing at Chicoutimi, where you can return along the opposite side of the fjord, picking up the HW138 again to follow it for another 200 km (125 miles) to Baie Comeau, passing lakes, forests and sandy inlets. A ferry crosses to Matane on the northern shores of the mountainous Gaspé Peninsula, where ravines cut through forested slopes and mountains tumble to a ragged coastline. This is superb motorcycle country, with enough riding and walking routes to occupy you for days. The road hugs the coastline around the peninsula, sometimes squeezing between the ocean and the mountains as it twists and turns. It passes picturesque coves and coastal villages, through the Parc National de Forillon and on to Gaspé Bay for fantastic ocean views to the point where, in 1534, French explorer Jacques Cartier 'discovered' the Gulf of St Lawrence which he named Canada.

◁ *The leisurely pace of this journey is well suited to its gentle landscape.*

▽ *The dramatic scenery of the Gaspé Peninsula.*

The Gulf of Maine to the Strait of Belle Isle

Follow the lovely Nova Scotia coast and journey to the remote Great Northern Peninsula of Newfoundland.

The North Atlantic will be your constant companion as you tour wild and remote Nova Scotia and Newfoundland. Cruise the Lighthouse Route through picturesque fishing villages and historic sea-faring towns, and ride the twisting and mountainous roads of the Cabot Trail for far-reaching ocean views. Discover the isolation and splendid natural beauty of Newfoundland as you ride alongside whales, seabirds and icebergs.

▽ *Cruising the Cabot Trail on Cape Breton Island.*

With over 7,000 km (4,350 miles) of winding coastal roads, there are plenty of opportunities to pull over and relax on a ride through Nova Scotia. The pace cranks up a notch in Newfoundland, as distances between towns are long and the weather is unpredictable. In both Nova Scotia and Newfoundland the North Atlantic weather takes its toll on the roads; do not expect perfect tarmac and make sure you pack your waterproofs. This route offers great riding, quiet roads and stunning natural beauty.

△ *Baddeck Bay on Cape Breton Island, Nova Scotia.*

The Route

The following route gives you a flavour of Nova Scotia and a taste of the vast island of Newfoundland. Two weeks will allow for time off the bike to explore the national parks.

The seaside town of Yarmouth is the starting point for the scenic Lighthouse Route, that follows the southern shore, hugging the coast for just under 600 km (373 miles). The riding is leisurely as you cruise into the historic port towns and fishing villages that line the route. The waters team with marine life, ensuring fresh seafood is brought in daily. What better way to end your day's ride than feasting upon lobster, tuna or mussels washed down with wines from the Annapolis Valley? The Lighthouse Route ends at the vibrant capital of Halifax.

Continue following the coast east of Halifax along HW7, which cuts inland after around 175 km (109 miles) heading north, then east to the Strait of Canso and the narrow causeway that links the rest of Nova Scotia to Cape Breton Island. The Cabot Trail is a stunningly scenic loop of 300 km (185 miles) around the northern tip of Cape Breton Island, encompassing woodland, soaring mountains, rocky cliffs and beaches as it skirts the edge of Cape Breton Highlands National Park. The highway is carved into the side of mountains; wide sweeping bends rise and dip, affording amazing views of the Atlantic Ocean and the Gulf of St Lawrence.

Leaving the Cabot Trail, an hour's ride takes you to North Sydney for the 14 hour ferry trip to Newfoundland. The locals simply call it 'The Rock'. You land in Argentia on the southwest corner of the Avalon Peninsula and take the beautiful 400 km (249 mile) loop that skirts the coast around the Avalon Wilderness Reserve. The rich waters of Bay Bulls and Witless Bay team with humpback and minke whales and millions of seabirds; occasionally icebergs drift into view. Head towards the capital, St John's, and nearby Cape Spear, the easternmost place on the North American continent. From St John's get on the Trans-Canada Highway – the only main road running across the island's northern shore. The road cuts across the Terra Nova National Park and through the towns of Gander and Grand Falls for almost 600 km

▷ *A HOG (Harley Owners' Group) rally in Cape Breton.*

▽ *Gros Morne National Park, Newfoundland.*

(373 miles) to Deer Lake, where you turn off onto Route 430 and the Viking Trail, which runs north for 489 km (304 miles). Enjoy the ride as fast, sweeping roads take you through Gros Morne National Park, a UNESCO World Heritage Site. The road leads to the moonscape of the Tablelands, a stunning glacier-carved fjord, and down to the water's edge at Rocky Harbour. The Viking Trail continues north to the Strait of Belle Isle and the remains of an 11th century Norse colony at L'Anse aux Meadows, on the tip of the northern peninsula. As you stand next to your motorcycle looking out to sea, it isn't hard to imagine those Viking longships riding the winds on this wild, rugged coastline.

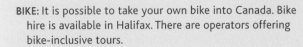

BIKE: It is possible to take your own bike into Canada. Bike hire is available in Halifax. There are operators offering bike-inclusive tours.

WEATHER WATCH: Weather is unpredictable, even in the summer months. It can be warm and sunny as well as cool, wet, windy and foggy. It's likely to be a little of everything, so prepare accordingly.

EXTENDING THE RIDE: Get the ferry from Yarmouth to Portland, Maine for a ride around New England, or ride through New Brunswick to the Gaspé Peninsula in Quebec.

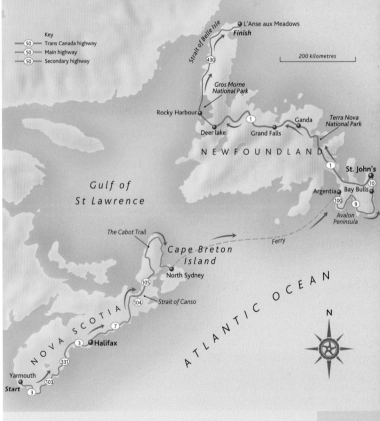

Boston to the Green Mountains

From Boston ride north along the Gulf of Maine, then head inland to the White Mountains of New Hampshire and the Green Mountains of Vermont.

If you enjoy riding on crisp, autumn mornings, when that chill in the air seems to make your bike run so much more smoothly, and a late sunrise slowly illuminates the changing colour of the trees, then head to New England for what has to be one of the world's finest natural displays. The forests of Maine, Vermont and New Hampshire put on a flamboyant autumn show of fiery red maples and brilliant yellow birches, aspen and poplars. The spectrum of colour is intense and highlighted beautifully by the changing autumn skies.

▽ *Motoring along the roads of New England.*

An extravaganza of changing colour combined with twisting mountain roads, rolling hills and a relaxed pace of life has to make this the ultimate autumn ride. These rural states just lend themselves to laid-back and lazy riding, and accommodation options are plentiful. A fun way to catch the headline acts in this spectacular show is to follow the daily bulletins and leave the planning of your route to Mother Nature, but if you prefer to combine catching the colours with some of New England's finest motorcycle roads, then some pre-planning ensures an amazing ride.

The Route

Spend a week following a route that combines coastal riding in Maine with rural roads that sweep through mountainous forests.

North of Boston, HW1 runs within a few kilometres of the coast, crossing the border into Maine just beyond Portsmouth. With no helmet laws in the state of Maine you can, if you wish, ride alongside the waves with the salt air on your face and through your hair. But be warned, the dramatic coastline can be wild and windswept! With numerous scenic roads leading from

HW1 to craggy coves, picturesque villages and historic towns, it is a laid-back coastal ride offering time to partake of the local seafood, particularly lobsters.

It is a beautiful 177 km (110 mile) ride from Boston to Portland, about halfway up the coast. From Portland head inland to Conway in New Hampshire, a ride of around 100 km (62 miles). Spend days meandering along the lazily winding roads within the White Mountain National Forest, where swathes of colour confront you at every turn. Once an area of wilderness, the forests of the White Mountains are one of the star turns of the annual display. As foliage rides go, the twisting Kancamagus Highway running between

▽ New England is famous for its dazzling displays of autumnal colour.

▷ *Beautiful rural Vermont, where this journey finishes.*

BIKE: It is possible to take your own bike into the USA. Bike hire is available in Boston and other major US cities. There are operators offering year-round bike-inclusive tours.

WEATHER WATCH: Autumn starts in the far north in September – moving south it runs to the end of October. Track the forecasts on one of the many websites devoted to the season, such as www.foliagenetwork.com.

EXTENDING THE RIDE: Ride from Vermont to Montreal in Quebec, or take a boat from Portland, Maine to Yarmouth in Nova Scotia.

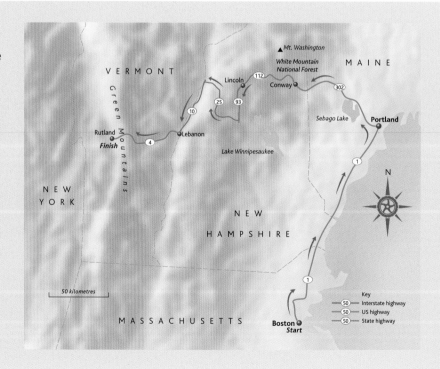

Conway and Lincoln is unbeatable. 'The Kank' is 55 km (34 miles) of sweeping views and spectacular sights, rising to almost 914 m (3,000 ft). At the height of autumn traffic can be slow, but the beauty of travelling by bike is the fun of leaving the queues behind. Within the park, the Mount Washington Auto Road is a 13 km (8 mile) climb of endless hairpins and breathtaking views up the east side of the mountain. Check your brakes before attempting the journey down!

Weave your way southwest to Lebanon near the Connecticut River, the natural border with Vermont. It is a superb 82 km (51 mile) ride along Route 4 from Lebanon to Rutland and the Green Mountain National Forest. Rural Vermont is covered by mountainous forests that exhibit a mesmerizing spectrum of colour. Its roads lead to sleepy hamlets of white, steepled churches and traditional country stores serving Vermont's speciality – maple syrup. Pull over for pancakes lavishly loaded with the sweetest syrup you have ever tasted, keeping your own engine running sweetly for hours.

▽ BELOW LEFT *Forests of gold are a common sight.*

▽ BELOW RIGHT *A river in the White Mountains.*

Denver to Durango via the Black Hills of South Dakota

Ride through Wyoming's wide open prairies, through the Black Hills and over mountain passes south to the lively town of Durango.

Colorado is the state of continuous curves, crystal clear lakes, cliffs and canyons. Clear mountain air, the smell of alpine forests and abundant wildlife make for an exhilarating ride. Contrast Colorado's mountain scenery with the emptiness of Wyoming's windswept prairies and the Black Hills of South Dakota, home to many Native Americans.

Enjoy blue skies, bright sunshine and magnificent mountain peaks as far as the eye can see as you negotiate hairpin bends on 3,650 m (12,000 ft) passes and ride Trail Ridge Road – the highest continuous paved road in the USA. Rumble over Red Mountain Pass on the

▽ *The Black Hills of South Dakota.*

'Million Dollar Highway' and, if you time it right, you can party with 100,000 other motorcyclists at Sturgis, the world's largest motorcycle rally.

△ *Join the party at the Sturgis Rally.*

The Route

If you only have a week, start in Denver then ride into the Rocky Mountain National Park and head south to Durango. If you can spare two weeks, head first into Wyoming and loop around the Black Hills before dropping back down to Colorado.

A 322 km (200 mile) ride north out of Denver across the plains brings you to Cheyenne and the world's largest outdoor rodeo. Consider staying the night, swap your helmet for a Stetson and your Sidis for a pair of cowboy boots and, if you are feeling really brave, exchange 70 bhp for one very raw bhp!

Leave town on HW25, following in the footsteps of the early pioneers as you ride across Wyoming's windswept, wide-open prairies, enjoying the sense of space as you edge open the throttle and ride into ancient Indian hunting grounds. Get onto the Iron Mountain Road, which spirals up the Black Hills of South Dakota. The road will take you on a scenic ride through Custer State Park, bringing you face-to-face with over 1,500 bison. Be prepared to stop if they decide to cross the road! The road then leads to Mount Rushmore

BIKE: It is possible to take your own bike into the USA. Bike hire is available in Denver. There are operators offering bike-inclusive tours.

WEATHER WATCH: June to mid-September is the best time to visit.

EXTENDING THE RIDE: Ride west to Monument Valley in Arizona or south to the Mexican border at El Paso.

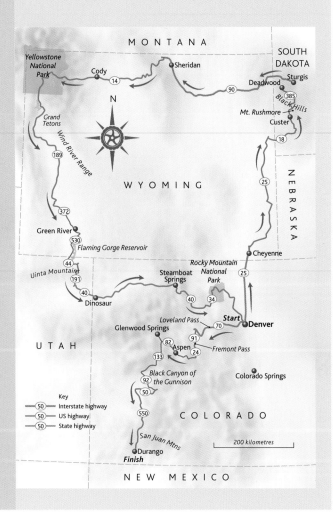

via scenic tunnels, where you can gaze upon the graven faces of four US presidents.

Head to nearby Deadwood, a frontier town with a wild past. Characters such as Wild Bill Hickock, Calamity Jane, Wyatt Earp and Doc Holliday once graced its saloons and established its infamous reputation. These days the town offers a wide range of accommodation and it makes a good base to explore the area. The town of Sturgis is just a short ride from Deadwood. If you are in the area in August, the Sturgis Rally has to be experienced. Started by the Jackpine Gypsies Motorcycle Club in 1938 with just nine racers, it is now one of the oldest and largest motorcycle events, attracting riders from all over the world. Enjoy a week of music, motorcycles and mayhem, swilling beer, swapping stories and partying with the wild and the weird.

If you partied too hard at Sturgis and feel the need for peace and tranquillity, then head west back into Wyoming and Yellowstone, the world's first national park. It's a long 450 km (280 mile) ride, so consider breaking the journey about halfway at the town of Sheridan. There are over 500 km (310 miles) of roads within Yellowstone leading to canyons, cliffs, geysers and hot springs. Enjoy the tranquillity and breathtaking beauty of this magnificent landscape. From the southern border of Yellowstone, ride south for around 410 km (255 miles) through the Grand Teton National Park and skirt the edges of the Wind River Range. The stretch of road to Green River provides magnificent views of jagged, snow-capped peaks as well as great riding. Spend the night in the city of Green River, rising early to wind your way east past Flaming Gorge Reservoir and over the Uinta Mountains to Dinosaur National Monument, where you cross back into Colorado. Steamboat Springs makes a good overnight halt after a day's ride of around 443 km (275 miles). This is where the serious sport of motorcycling along mountainous passes really begins. There are dozens of passes to play on, so don't forget to stop occasionally and give your clutch a rest while you admire the peaks. Trail Ridge Road in the Rocky Mountain National Park at over 3,650 m (12,000 ft) and 75 km (47 miles) in length is the highest continuous highway in the States. Ride high into an alpine world through mountain meadows, colourful tundra and aspen groves. There are plenty of stopping points to admire the far-reaching views and snap photos of you and your bike framed against a background of spectacular glaciers and snowfields.

From the Rocky Mountain National Park, drop back down to Denver for an overnight stop to check the tyres and oil the clutch in anticipation of riding even more mountain passes. Leaving Denver, head west over the Loveland Pass, followed closely by the Fremont Pass to the mountain town of Leadville and up over Independence Pass to Aspen.

If the glitz of Aspen is a little too much, then head northwest to Glenwood Springs for the night, where you can soak in the hot springs. From Glenwood Springs head southeast, skirting the north rim of the Black Canyon of the Gunnison and on to Ouray and the start of a ride along the 'Million Dollar Highway', which stretches for over 100 km (62 miles) to Durango. The ride through Uncompahgre Gorge to the summit of Red Mountain Pass consists of precipitous cliffs and hairpin bends as the road ascends the pass. Enjoy the buzz of the town of Durango while your bike cools down and the tyres stop steaming.

△ Riding past Mount Rushmore, South Dakota.

▽ The Million Dollar Highway en route to Durango, Colorado.

OVERLEAF Riding the roads around Sturgis.

The Wild West and the Californian Coast

Ride a circuit from Los Angeles through Arizona's Wild West, then across to Las Vegas in the Nevada desert. Head north to San Francisco, returning to Los Angeles via the Californian coast.

Grab the leading role in your own western and relive those classic John Wayne moments. Ride through Navajo and Apache lands, stop off at frontier towns and gaze down on the grandest canyon of them all. Arizona, Utah and Nevada represent America's west at its wildest. If names like Furnace Creek, Valley of the Gods and Hell's Backbone fire your imagination, then get your motor running and ride along roads that will have you grinning like Messrs Fonda and Hopper as you ride into the sunset.

▽ *The Grand Canyon National Park is well worth a few days' exploration.*

△ Big Sur, where the Santa Lucia Mountains rise abruptly from the Pacific Ocean.

Los Angeles makes a great starting point for a circular tour of switchbacks, sweeping curves, roads that disappear into the horizon and jaw-dropping scenery; not to mention historic sections of Route 66 and the Pacific coastline of HW1. If you want to get off-road for some of the route, the Great Western Trail (www.gwt.org) is a corridor of parallel trails traversing over 3,000 km (1,864 miles) of canyons, deserts, woodlands and forests, offering some truly adventurous riding. This region of the USA offers an extensive choice of riding terrains through incredible landscapes.

The Route

This route gives you a taste of the deserts of the Wild West, the glitz of Las Vegas and the superb Californian coast. Two weeks will allow for time off the bike in the national parks.

Leave Los Angeles and head east, motoring along original sections of Route 66 as far as Williams, Arizona – the gateway to the Grand Canyon National Park. Nothing can prepare you for the soaring, spectacular beauty of this place. Stay a few days and hike into the canyon to get a feel of the scale and solitude of one of the world's natural wonders.

A 270-km (167-mile) ride east through the rocky landscape of the Painted Desert and into Navajo territory takes you to Monument Valley. This is where the west was won – at least in

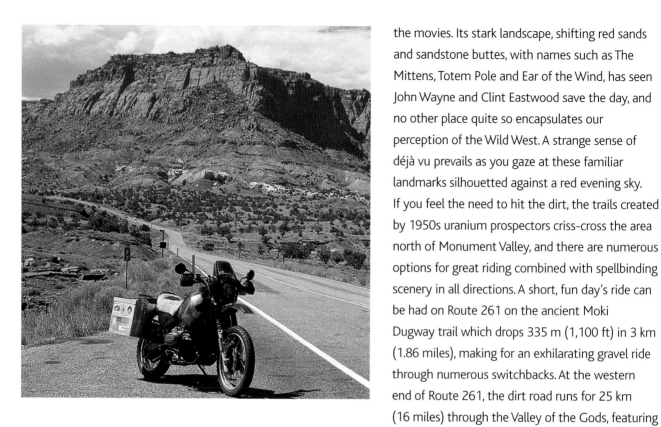

△ *Capitol Reef National Park, Utah.*

▷ *Yosemite National Park is famous for its spectacular granite cliffs, waterfalls and giant sequoia groves.*

the movies. Its stark landscape, shifting red sands and sandstone buttes, with names such as The Mittens, Totem Pole and Ear of the Wind, has seen John Wayne and Clint Eastwood save the day, and no other place quite so encapsulates our perception of the Wild West. A strange sense of déjà vu prevails as you gaze at these familiar landmarks silhouetted against a red evening sky. If you feel the need to hit the dirt, the trails created by 1950s uranium prospectors criss-cross the area north of Monument Valley, and there are numerous options for great riding combined with spellbinding scenery in all directions. A short, fun day's ride can be had on Route 261 on the ancient Moki Dugway trail which drops 335 m (1,100 ft) in 3 km (1.86 miles), making for an exhilarating gravel ride through numerous switchbacks. At the western end of Route 261, the dirt road runs for 25 km (16 miles) through the Valley of the Gods, featuring isolated sandstone columns which, according to the Navajo, are petrified warriors.

Leaving Monument Valley, head northwest on HW276, which crosses the Colorado River to link up with an impressive road (HW24) that skirts the southern tip of Capitol Reef National Park. Head south to Boulder City on HW12 and then take the ride of your life on a 60 km (38 mile) stretch across the top of the Aquarius Plateau. Hell's Backbone is a hair-raising ride with sheer drops to Sand Creek and Death Hollow on either side. The views are stupendous as the dirt road climbs up and around Box Death Hollow Wilderness below and crosses a narrow bridge. At Escalante return to HW12 and ride along a road blasted through the rocks to Bryce Canyon. As evening approaches, the changing light plays on the canyon's hoodoos (tall thin spires of rock), providing an almost psychedelic, technicolour display of the weird and wonderful landscape, providing a magical end to an exhilarating day's ride. From here it is just over an hour's scenic ride to Zion National Park, a welcome oasis with its cascading waterfalls. Relax and wash off the desert dust in the cool waters on the Emerald Pools Trail.

Just 90 km (56 miles) southwest of Zion is Las Vegas, a city of fantasy shimmering in the desert. Enter the world of 24-hour entertainment, Elvis impersonators and the infamous Las

Vegas Strip. Once you've had your fill of fantasy, load up your bike and roar out of town in the early morning light into the Mojave Desert and Death Valley, descending below sea level into desolate and dramatic scenery. It is claimed to be the hottest place on Earth, so slake your thirst at Furnace Creek and ride out to Dante's View before hitting the switchbacks and mountain passes leading north to Mammoth Lakes and Yosemite National Park. In Yosemite ride over the Tioga Pass, which threads through alpine meadows along the spine of the Sierra Nevada. A 300 km (186 mile) ride from Yosemite through Gold Country brings you to the beautiful city of San Francisco. Relax for a few days and appreciate its charms before hitting HW1 for the 644 km (400 mile) ride to Big Sur and on to Los Angeles. This is a fantastic finale to your journey through the Wild West. The coastal breeze will blow away the last of the desert sand as you cruise down a highway that hugs the rugged coast along the Pacific Ocean. The coastline is fringed by lighthouses, crumbling cliffs, soft white sand and giant redwoods. With a big, blue Californian sky above and a turquoise ocean as far as the eye can see, relax into the ride and enjoy some easy living. The surf is spectacular and there are enough sweeping curves and tight turns to keep the riding sweet until you swing into Los Angeles.

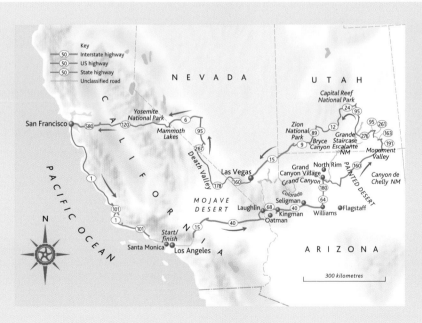

BIKE: It is possible to take your own bike into the USA. Las Vegas, Los Angeles and Phoenix all offer a wide choice of bike hire. There are operators offering bike-inclusive tours.

WEATHER WATCH: The best time to visit is September to mid-October, or April and May for desert wild flowers. Avoid summer's baking desert temperatures.

EXTENDING THE RIDE: From Los Angeles follow Route 66 west as far as Albuquerque, then head north to Durango for a ride in the Colorado Rockies.

tool box

Route 66: Flagstaff to Los Angeles

Route 66 crosses the country from Chicago to Los Angeles for 3,939 km (2,448 miles) through eight states. It is still possible to follow much of the original road and, in doing so, relive a little of America's recent history.

▽ *Motorcycle journeys in the US can be epic in scale, so take frequent breaks and enjoy the ride.*

Perhaps one of the most famous roads in the world, Route 66 has been immortalized in music, literature and on screen. Fondly referred to as the Mother Road, it was established in 1926 and ran from Chicago to Los Angeles. In the 1930s the road transported immigrants in search of a better life to sunny, golden California. By 1937 it was fully paved, becoming the main military route during the Second World War. In the 1950s it

◁ *Old gas bowsers along Route 66.*

▽ *The iconic Route 66, which historically ran from Chicago to LA.*

was the road taken by holidaymakers heading to the west coast. Roadside attractions and fast-food joints sprang up along the way to cater to the passing trade, until eventually the road itself became part of the vacation. Although officially decommissioned in 1985, the spirit of the road in its heyday lives on.

This motorcycle journey is not about negotiating hairpin bends or climbing high for spectacular views; in fact much of the original highway was flat. It is more a journey into a state of mind, a motorcycle ride through history following a road that represented freedom and adventure. Whatever your preferred ride, perhaps, just this once, a Harley Davidson is the motorcycle to ride on this celebrated route. Ride an American machine as you follow the road that epitomizes the American Dream.

The Route

Riding the full length of Route 66 would probably take around three weeks. The following route can be ridden in a couple of days and covers the final section from Flagstaff in Arizona to Los Angeles, along some of the best surviving stretches of the original road, where classic petrol stations, motels and diners evoke everything you have ever heard about this classic road.

Pick up a hire bike in Phoenix, then head north on Interstate 17 for about 225 km (140 miles) to Flagstaff. Around 40 km (25 miles) west of Flagstaff is the town of Williams,

BIKE: It is possible to take your own bike into the USA. Bike hire is available in Phoenix and Los Angeles. There are operators offering bike-inclusive tours.

WEATHER WATCH: April to October is a good time to visit, but be prepared for Arizona's baking summer temperatures.

EXTENDING THE RIDE: Incorporate this ride into a trip through Arizona's Wild West.

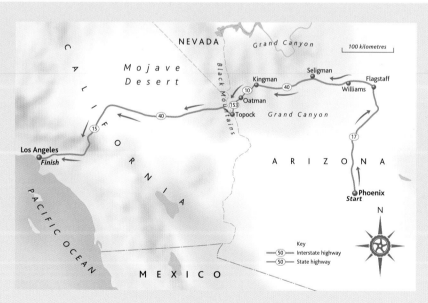

gateway to the Grand Canyon, and historically the last town to have its section of the Mother Road bypassed. Park up at one of the classic 1950s diners or try an ice-cream soda at Twisters Soda Fountain.

A short ride west brings you to the village of Ash Fork and the start of around 260 km (162 miles) of the original Route 66. Open up the throttle as you motor across open plains to Seligman, another classic Route 66 town. Check out the barbershop of Angel Delgadillo, the founding member of the association to preserve the Mother Road. His barbershop walls are lined with business cards and stickers from passing clients. Continuing west, the road dips through rolling countryside affording expansive views. This is the open road and the Harley is in her element, that familiar throaty rumble of the engine filling the air. Fill up at the gas station at Hackberry, its forecourt a colourful reminder of 1950s America. Southwest of Kingman the road starts to climb into the Black Mountains, and the most enjoyable riding of the route. Ease on that lazy Harley power and glide along the narrow road as it snakes and twists through the mountains, climbing through canyons towards Oatman. Once a gold-mining centre, these days the dusty streets are filled with creaky saloons and roaming donkeys.

From Oatman the road descends towards Topock and the Californian border. The cool mountains give way to a dry heat and dramatic landscape as you approach Los Angeles through the Mojave Desert. Cruise into town heading for the Santa Monica Pier. Cut the engine, gaze across the Pacific Ocean and reflect on your once-in-a-lifetime ride along this iconic road.

◁ *The road through the Black Mountains.*

▽ *Los Angeles – the end of the road.*

The Sierra Madres Mountains to the Pacific Coast

Ride from the Rio Grande across the Chihuahua Desert, through the canyons of the Sierra Madres Mountains and over the Devil's Backbone to the warm waters of the Pacific Coast.

Northern Mexico is a region of mountains, desert, giant cacti and sleepy, dusty towns where spicy tortillas are washed down with tequila and moustachioed Mariachi bands play at week-long fiestas. Folklore and magic rituals interweave with the Catholicism of the conquistadors, and the history of the region echoes with stories of the Mexican Revolution. The skies are brilliant blue, the beer is cold and the warmth and kindness of the Mexican people will surprise you.

▽ *There are six separate canyons in the Copper Canyon system.*

The motorcycling possibilities are endless, and you will be amazed by the varied terrain and choice of riding. You can cruise the highways on a sports bike; the toll roads are expensive but well surfaced and fast; or take a dual sport machine and brave the dirt roads, to really get a flavour of Mexico's natural beauty.

The Route

This route can easily be ridden in a week. Allow a little longer if you plan on including some sightseeing.

Crossing into Mexico over the Rio Grande from El Paso, Texas you hit the arid rocky deserts of Mexico's north, the landscape characterized by giant Saguaro cacti and, after the summer rains, stunning desert wildflowers. A fast five-hour ride south through the desert on HW45 brings you to the lively city of Chihuahua, synonymous with the Mexican Revolution and the life of Mexico's hero Pancho Villa. His home is now the Museo de la Revolución Mexicana.

BIKE: It is possible to take your own bike into Mexico. Bike hire in San Antonio, Texas or Phoenix, Arizona is recommended. There are operators offering bike-inclusive tours.

WEATHER WATCH: It is a year-round destination but expect chilly nights from November to February.

EXTENDING THE RIDE: Ride north to Phoenix from where you can join the final section of Route 66, or take a ride through Arizona's Wild West.

It is a fun, twisting 230 km (143 miles) south along HW16 to Creel, a mountain town perched at 2,300 m (7,546 ft) and surrounded by pine-covered mountains. Creel makes a good base for visiting Copper Canyon, the name given to network of mammoth canyons which cut through the Sierra Madre range. As dirt roads are upgraded, an increasing network of roads now connect the canyons. Dirt bikers can enjoy the off-road trails and road bikes can follow the 50 km (31 mile) paved road running along the rim

Key
50 Motorway
50 National road
— Main road
— Minor road

◁ *Durango was once a popular location for shooting movies.*

of Copper Canyon from Creel to Divisadero. Lodges perch on the edge of the canyon offering truly spectacular views – stay the night to experience the stunning sunset and the enveloping silence.

You can leave your bike for a few days and trek into the canyon, or ride the dirt road to the village of Batopilas which lies at the bottom. It is a thrilling 150 km (93 mile) ride from Creel on a partly paved but mainly dirt road that switchbacks and twists its way to the ravine below, descending nearly 1,500 m (5,000 ft) through dramatic scenery. Depending on your off-road experience, it can take three to six hours to complete the descent. At 495 m (1,624 ft), Batopilas' climate is distinctly warmer, where tropical fruit thrives and the streets are lined with bougainvillea.

The same road climbs out of the canyon back to Creel, whence you head south on HW23 for 130 km (81 miles) to Guachochi along a road that skirts the edge of the canyons, continuing for a further 190 km (119 miles) through cactus-strewn mountain scenery to Hidalgo del Parral, infamous as the site of Pancho Villa's assassination. A brief stay is recommended to enjoy this charming, mellow town with narrow winding streets.

Join HW45 for the fast 410 km (255 mile) ride to Durango, a cowboy town and once a popular movie location. There are plenty of hotels and restaurants, and the leafy square is a great place to pull over and sit in the shade near the cool fountains. About 160 km (99 miles) west of Durango you hit the spectacular stretch of road called El Espinazo del Diablo (Devil's Backbone), which narrows and twists for about 170 km (106 miles) through high pines and rugged scenery before descending to tropical vegetation as you ride south of the Tropic of Cancer to the palm-fringed beaches of Mazatlán.

◁ FAR LEFT *Finding a shady spot en route to the coast at Mazatlán.*

▽ *Cacti in northern Mexico.*

San José Circuit

Ride north from San José through the lush Central Valley, then head south to the idyllic beaches of the Pacific before returning to the capital.

△ *Make sure you leave time to enjoy Costa Rica's idyllic beaches.*

Tiny Costa Rica is Central America made simple; a safe and peaceful paradise bordered by the warm waters of the Pacific and the Caribbean. Costa Rica's uniqueness lies in its variety of landscapes, colourful wildlife and climate zones. Relax on tropical beaches where the rainforest spills onto the sand, step into an enchanted world on canopy walks that swing through the cloud forest, and watch in awe as active volcanoes illuminate the night sky.

Distances are short, with nowhere more than a long day's ride from the capital. The road network is extensive but varied, with short stretches of dual carriageway leading out of the capital but then branching off to single-track potholed roads and gravel trails. It is possible to stick to a combination of highways and paved roads, just occasionally tackling a dirt road. Alternatively spend the whole journey ripping along the network of single trails; a challenging combination of dirt, sand and gravel. Riding in Costa Rica is fantastic fun and the choice of riding terrain is entirely up to you.

The Route

This classic one-week route connects some of Costa Rica's most famous highlights, riding a mixture of paved and dirt roads.

From San José head northwest through the Central Valley to the town of Alajuela. The views are stunning as the small, paved road climbs through fruit farms and coffee plantations up the slopes of the Poás Volcano. Walk along a path that leads around the crater rim for views into its steaming lagoon.

Continue northwest via narrow, paved roads that wind through gorgeous valleys to Fortuna, gateway to the Arenal National Park and the Volcán Arenal, a classic cone-shaped active volcano that regularly emits rock bombs and fiery orange lava. There are ample places to stay in the area, so unpack the bike and join one of the late-afternoon treks through the rainforest, concluding in an evening bathe in the Tabaçon hot springs. Lounge in the thermal waters, listen to the volcanic rumblings and watch the night-time display. From Fortuna head west along the R142, a bumpy road that skirts around the northern edge of Arenal Lake for 40 km (25 miles) to Tilaran, where you pick up a rough dirt road for a further 40 km (25 miles) to the beautiful cloud-forest reserve of Monteverde. Road conditions get rough – loose gravel with some big rocks – but the views over mountains and valleys are stupendous, so take your time and enjoy the ride. Spend at least a day exploring the luxuriant vegetation at Monteverde, which is home to an astounding variety of wildlife. Stroll across suspended walkways for a monkey's-eye view of the steaming rainforest, or observe the activity from the saddle of a horse.

▽ *The Arenal Volcano is still active, and last had a major eruption in 2000.*

COSTA RICA

tool box

BIKE: It is possible to take your own bike into Costa Rica. Bike hire is available in San Jose. There are operators offering bike-inclusive tours.

WEATHER WATCH: December to mid-May is the dry season. Rains are heaviest between June and October.

EXTENDING THE RIDE: No overland connection to other featured journeys.

Tilarán
Laguna de Arenal
R142
Arenal
Fortuna
Puerto Viejo de Sarapiquí
Arenal National Park
Santa Elena
Ciudad Quesada (San Carlos)
R4
Las Juntas
Monteverde
R9
R145
Volcan Poás National Park
Barva
Miramar
San Ramón
Alajuela
HW1
San José
Start/finish
Barranca
Colón
27
Orotina
Santiago
Rio Tárcoles
San Ignacio de Acosta
N
34
Santa Maria
PACIFIC OCEAN
239
Quepos
25 kilometres
Manuel Antonio National Park

Key
50 — Motorway
50 — National road
50 — Main road
— Minor road

78

Leaving Monteverde, it is a full day's ride of around 160 km (99 miles) to the coast. Some 35 km (22 miles) of challenging and twisting dirt roads and spectacular views await you, before you pick up the Pan-American Highway near the town of Las Juntas. Head south, branching off at Barranca towards the Pacific Coast. As you ride over the Rio Tarcoles, pull over to spot crocodiles resting on the muddy banks below. The road conditions on this section are variable, with reasonable tarmac giving way to large potholes, as you ride south to Quepos and the beautiful beaches and incredible flora and fauna of the Manuel Antonio National Park. Explore the surrounding mountain ranges along gravel trails, see the wildlife up close and relax on the white, sandy beaches. There are several routes leading from the coast into the mountains and back to San José, a journey of around 160 km (99 miles). The most scenic route leads from Quepos via Santa Maria de Dota, but can only be done in the dry season and requires good off-road skills. A slightly easier gravel route goes from Paquera via San Igancio de Acosta, and from there on smaller, paved highways back to San José. Alternatively take the paved road north to Jaco via Orotina and finally westbound back to San José, a reasonably fast route taking around four to five hours. This is the beauty of riding in Costa Rica – short distances, constantly changing scenery and a fun and varied choice of riding terrain.

◁ FAR LEFT *Loaded and ready to go.*

◁ LEFT *Getting into the swing of the local culture.*

▽ *Enjoying the view from the Monteverde road.*

Patagonia: Journey to the End of the World

Ride from Temuco in Chile to Ushuaia, the capital of the Argentine province of Tierra del Fuego, and the world's southernmost city.

Riding down through Patagonia to Tierra del Fuego at the tip of South America, it can really feel like you are approaching the end of the Earth. Whilst the northern part is a land of lakes and snow-capped peaks with an almost European, alpine appearance, as you travel southwards the scenery and weather become wilder and the population centres smaller and further apart. Patagonia is the area of South America lying below 37 degrees south and consists of both Chilean and Argentinean territory. You will find yourself crossing the two frontiers many times, but this is very straightforward with few delays being encountered at customs. Campsites and inexpensive hotels are easily found along the route.

▽ *The stunning scenery in the Torres del Paine National Park.*

△ *The Patagonian Lake District in Chile, where this journey begins.*

The Andes run the whole length of the western side of South America, and you will cross back and forth over them several times on your journey – one of the highlights as the twisting roads take you from one side to the other. Then you come to the famous Ruta 40, hundreds of kilometres of gravel road where you can be blown off course and buffeted constantly by the strong winds sweeping across Patagonia. You will soon get used to riding your bike leaning at an angle. It is possible to avoid sections of this road and keep more to sealed routes if you wish.

The Route

Allow two to three weeks to complete the journey, allowing time for sightseeing and time out from riding.

Begin your journey in Temuco in Chilean Patagonia, an area known as the 'Lake District'. Heading southeast towards the Andes, it is a short ride of 112 km (70 miles) to the towns of Villarica and Pucon, the start of a region of huge lakes and snow-capped volcanoes. The smooth, paved road twists its way alongside a deep blue lake with the

△ *The Perito Moreno Glacier is still advancing.*

Volcan Villarica as your backdrop. It is possible to walk up this snowy peak and peer down into its crater, the glowing lava and sulphurous smoke rising up towards you. Travel on good dirt roads past giant pine forests and lakes in the Villarica National Park for 87 km (54 miles) to the Argentinean frontier.

Heading down the other side of the mountains, you will ride on a combination of dirt and sealed roads which will take you past many lakes. After around 200 km (125 miles) you finally reach a perfect, winding sealed road for your run into to Bariloche, the last 20 km (12 miles) hugging the shore of Lago Nahuel Huapi. Bariloche itself is a very Swiss-looking town and ski resort beautifully situated on the shore of the lake, and is the centre for outdoor activities in the area such as hiking and trout fishing. From here the winding and narrow sealed road heads south for 260 km (160 miles), running past more stunning scenery which then opens up into rolling hills as you approach the town of Esquel. The last 100 km (62 miles) are on the infamous Ruta 40 and it can be extremely windy, so be careful not to get blown off the road. You really feel you are in wild Patagonia from here on down; southwards from here the roads are entirely gravel or dirt embedded with rocks. The Andes will be to your right from now on and contain the largest glaciers outside the Polar region. This is the land of the *gauchos* (cowboys), and the only indication of habitation are signs by the entrance roads to huge *estancias* (cattle farms). Keep your wheels running in the ruts in the gravel left by other vehicles and try to avoid being blown into the pile of stones along the centre – often several inches deep.

OVERLEAF *Baralacha La, on the Manali to Leh road.*

There are some great side trips not to be missed on the way down. Once you reach Tres Lagos 520 km (323 miles) from Chile Chico, turn off Ruta 40 and take a dirt road for 150 km

(93 miles) to the small settlement of El Chalten in the Fitzroy National Park. From here, short treks are possible to see stupendous views of Cerro Fitzroy and Cerro Torre.

Return back to the junction and turn off after 100 km (62 miles) to El Calafate, from where you can ride down to see the immense Perito Moreno Glacier, one of the few in the world that is actually advancing. You can stand and watch 60 m (197 ft) high pieces of ice fall away from the 5 km (3 miles) wide snout and plunge into the vivid blue lake.

Retrace your route back to join Ruta 40 and head back south for 200 km (124 miles) through Cerro Castillo to Puerto Natales in Chile. The road is still unsealed and you will see guanacos (a relative of the llama), possibly condors and even flamingos on the salt flats near the border. It is well worth riding into the Torres del Paine National Park along a good dirt road, with truly wonderful views of the Torres themselves and the Cuernos del Paine towering above the lake as you ride around the opposite bank.

Cut back east to ride 200 km (124 miles) across desolate windswept pampas back into Argentina, passing old ruined settlements to reach the town of Rio Gallegos and the end of Ruta 40. From here on you need to take Ruta 3. Head south, cross back into Chile and take the ferry the short distance over the Strait of Magellan to the island of Tierra del Fuego, itself divided between both Argentina and Chile, a wild land of stunning lakes, forests and mountain scenery. From the ferry you can see your final destination – the Argentinean town of Ushuaia – 450 km (280 miles) away. Situated on the Beagle Channel, it was named in 1832 by Charles Darwin after his ship. The town is a departure point for ships to Antarctica and can be quite busy when they are in port. There is only one last thing to do at the end of your long ride. Travel a few kilometres out of town to the end of the road until you can go no further. After some long, tough riding you have finally reached the end of the world – *el fin del mundo*.

BIKE: It is possible to take your own bike into Chile. You can hire bikes in Osorno. There are operators offering bike-inclusive tours.

WEATHER WATCH: December to March is really the only time to ride this route by motorcycle.

EXTENDING THE RIDE: No overland connection to other featured journeys.

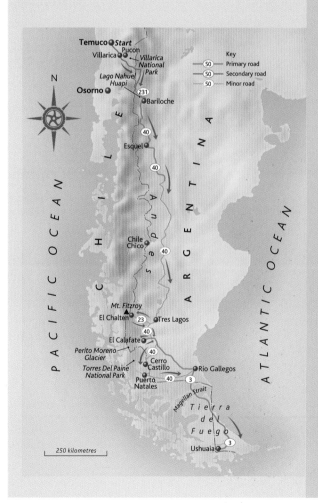

Colombo Circuit

Ride north from Colombo to the Cultural Triangle, dropping slightly south to the central hill country before returning to Colombo on roads that wind through tea plantations.

△ *Buddhist cave temples at Dambulla.*

The island of Sri Lanka is a beautiful paradise of idyllic beaches, thick jungles and highlands swathed with tea plantations. Ancient Buddhist art can be found in cave temples and ancient cities, while the colossal rock fortress at Sigiriya rises from the rainforest, affording spectacular views. The landscape is stunning and the food is delicious, but it is the warm welcome and genuine kindness of the Sri Lankan people that stays with you long after leaving the 'Island of Serendipity'.

Travelling by motorcycle has to be one of the best ways to appreciate the gorgeous scenery here. The road surfaces are not great and potholes litter even the main roads, but the pace of traffic is fairly slow. Distances between places of interest are short and, if you want to blow the budget, there are some fabulous places to stay. This is a relaxed motorcycle trip where you can ride for a day through lovely countryside, find a tranquil base and spend a few days exploring the surrounding countryside.

The Route

Ten days for the following route allows for a two- to three-night stay in each region.

Get an early start out of Colombo before the traffic gets too frantic. The 148 km (91 mile) ride north to Dambulla, at the heart of the Cultural Triangle, is short but the main two-lane highway is busy and uneven in places as the road winds through a verdant countryside of paddy fields, banana plantations and coconut palms. Dambulla makes a good base for exploring the sights of the Cultural Triangle, which is littered with the remains of ancient palaces and cities. Don't be too surprised if you see wild elephants wandering across the road – it goes without saying that they have the right of way! At Dambulla visit the Buddhist cave temples then take a 25 km (14 mile) ride north to the magnificent citadel of Sigiriya, towering above the plains atop a 200 m (656 ft) rocky outcrop.

The following day, take a 68 km (42 mile) ride to the ancient capital of Polonnaruwa, where temples, palaces and sculptures nestle in the surrounding woodland. Leaving the Cultural Triangle, head out on the A9 towards Kandy and the hill country. Run the gauntlet of spice merchants whose gardens line the road near Matale, then drop down through green hills to the lovely lakeside city of Kandy, another great base for a few days. Visit Buddha's Tooth, ride out to the botanical gardens and take a day trip to the Pinnewala Elephant Orphanage just 40 km (25 miles) west of Kandy. Their bath time in the Oya River is not to be missed.

▽ *Kandy is one of the most scenic cities in Sri Lanka.*

Leaving Kandy, the 77 km (47 mile) ride into the hill country is incredibly scenic but also unforgettably bumpy, making the ride fairly slow going. Break the journey with a visit to one of the tea estates you will pass along the way, and stay for the after-tour tea and cake. Step back in time as you approach the old British hill town of Nuwara Eliya, where you can stay in hotels that appear little changed since the turn of the century. This is the heart of the tea industry and the surrounding countryside is beautiful. Take a scenic 30 km (19 mile) ride out to Horton Plains National Park, a rugged high-altitude moorland, where the dramatic escarpment of World's End plunges through mists to the plains.

From Nuwara Eliya weave your way back to Colombo along possibly the most stunning road of the trip – the A7, which winds for 180 km (111 miles) through lush forest and tea plantations, every turn revealing breathtaking views. Spend your last evening in Sri Lanka strolling along Galle Face Green, the oceanfront promenade, alive with street food vendors and families enjoying the balmy ocean breeze.

tool box

BIKE: Getting your own bike into Sri Lanka is not straightforward. Bike hire is available in Negombo. There are operators offering bike-inclusive tours.

WEATHER WATCH: December to April is the best time to visit, but expect rain at any time of the year.

EXTENDING THE RIDE: No overland connection to other featured journeys.

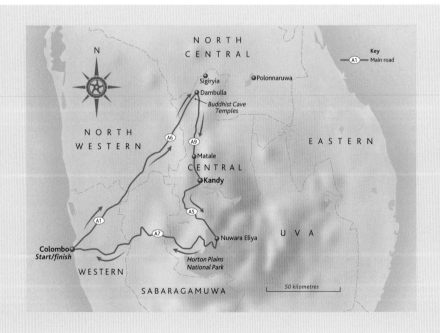

◁ FAR LEFT *The start of a fun day's ride.*

◁ *Exploring the dirt roads in Sri Lanka.*

▽ *A tea plantation near Nuwara Eliya.*

Delhi to Jaisalmer

*From Delhi, take a ride through the state of Rajasthan
to Jaisalmer in the Great Thar Desert.*

▽ BELOW LEFT *Jewel-
coloured saris glow
against the dusty land.*

▽ BELOW RIGHT *The camel
fair in Pushkar.*

The desert state of Rajasthan is the India of sandstone fortresses, architecturally intricate *havelis* (enclosed dwellings), turbaned and moustachioed men and beautiful, brightly dressed tribal women. For extremes of colour against a sparse, desert landscape and as in introduction to the Indian subcontinent, Rajasthan is hard to beat. Consider blowing the budget and spending at least one night in a converted palace.

Riding in India is a nerve-jangling, death-defying experience and not for the faint-hearted. Size really does matter on Indian roads, so be prepared to pull onto the dirt to let oncoming trucks go past, or to avoid sleeping cows. The main roads can be bone-shaking but, despite the mayhem, riding in India is great fun and an emotional rollercoaster. Tears of frustration can turn to laughter in minutes, as there is always something to make you smile. The people you meet and the things you see ensure that there will never be a dull day's ride. Traffic, livestock and humanity compete for space in the cities but, once out on the open road, rural India is magical. If you are picking up a bike in India it has to be the Enfield Bullet, a classic motorcycle designed in the 1950s and still produced in Madras. The brakes are poor and the suspension basic, but spares and mechanics are widespread and the pace, sound and feel is perfectly in tune with the surroundings. The Bullet is temperamental, indestructible and in her element on the Indian roads.

The Route

Allow two weeks for this journey as there is much to see, and a ride in India is so much more enjoyable if you are not in a rush; the fun of riding in India is in the journey itself.

As with any journey in India, try to leave early when the air is cool and the country is slowly awakening, so ride out of Delhi at first light before the traffic mayhem begins. The 260 km (162 mile) run southwest to Jaipur is along a fairly fast, busy road littered with potholes, so

△ ABOVE LEFT *There's always room for one more!*

△ ABOVE RIGHT *A chai stand in the Great Thar Desert.*

91

tool box

BIKE: It is possible to take your own bike into India. Bike hire or buy back schemes are available in Delhi. There are operators offering bike-inclusive tours.

WEATHER WATCH: November to February is the best time to visit. Avoid summer's baking temperatures.

EXTENDING THE RIDE: From Delhi, ride north to Ladakh.

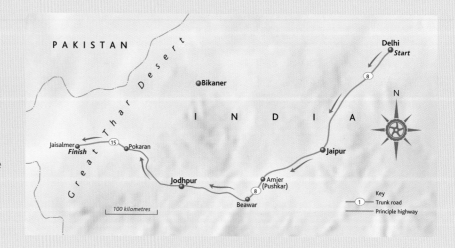

you'll need to have your wits about you. Lorries and buses career past belching diesel fumes in their wake, and your sooty face will amuse hotel-owners throughout your journey. Spend your first few nights in the pink city of Jaipur, visiting the myriad palaces, temples and bazaars in and around it. It is just under 150 km (93 miles) southwest to Pushkar, but average speeds are low on India's rural roads. Throughout your journey there will always be a chai stand by the side of the road offering sweet tea and respite from the heat and dust. Another favourite is the omelette stands, great for a mid-morning snack if you got on the road at dawn, but watch out for the chillies! Try to visit Pushkar in November when it hosts the annual Camel Fair. Rajasthani villagers travel in droves to the town, bringing camels and livestock to sell and race. Women leave their homes dressed in their finest clothes to buy bangles and silks, and visit the temples. It is an amazing experience and you will quickly get caught up in the excitement.

From Pushkar it is a dusty 200 km (124 mile) ride west to Jodhpur on the fringe of the Great Thar Desert, and you will probably be sharing the road with camel and buffalo carts. Jodhpur is dominated by the mighty Meherangarh Fort. Get up onto the ramparts for far-reaching views over the blue and white houses of the city and to the desert beyond. From Jodphur head 300 km (186 miles) west to Jaisalmer in India's remote western corner. It is a long, hot, dusty ride but the final approach to Jaisalmer is a spectacular sight, as the honey-coloured sandstone ramparts of Jaisalmer fort rise out of the desert plains. Lose yourself in the narrow streets, join a camel trek and take a ride out to the sand dunes at Sam on the edge of the Thar Desert. India is a riding experience like no other, requiring concentration, patience and, above all, a sense of humour. Hang on to this and you will have the ride of your life.

△ *Palace of the Winds, Jaipur.*

◁ *Meherangarh Fort, Jodhpur.*

▽ *Enfield Bullet, Jaisalmer.*

Manali to Leh

Ride from Manali in the fertile valleys of Himachal Pradesh, through remote valleys and on to the Tibetan Plateau and finally to Leh, in the Kingdom of Ladakh.

▽ *The Gata Loops, a series of spectacular hairpins.*

Perched on the northern tip of India, this Shangri-La of Tibetan Buddhism nestles between the towering mountain ranges of the Himalaya and the Karakoram. Once an important crossroads on the Silk Route between Central and Southeast Asia, Ladakh was then closed to foreigners until 1974. These days the weather conditions seal Ladakh from the outside world until the summer months, when the snow is cleared and we are allowed a glimpse of this legendary land.

It is now possible to ride to this remote and beautiful mountain kingdom on the legendary Manali to Leh Highway. Your incredible journey will take you past snow-capped peaks and ancient Lamaist monasteries clinging to sheer rock faces. It is a rollercoaster of a ride through a beautiful and austere landscape. Hairpin bends wind skywards over the high-altitude passes you must traverse to reach the fabled city of Leh. The road is single-track, with a surface that switches from tarmac to rough scree and rubble throughout the journey. Landslides and broken bridges are common and potholes fill with water and mud. Road conditions differ each year as extreme weather conditions take their toll, but it is one of the most scenic roads in the world and a ride along this highway is an unforgettable experience.

△ ABOVE LEFT *Reaching Khardung La.*

△ ABOVE RIGHT *Prayer flags are a common sight in this corner of the world.*

The Route

The road from Manali to Leh is one of the world's highest passable roads and weaves for almost 500 km (311 miles) over 4,000 m (131,23 ft) passes. The following journey includes two overnight stops, allowing time to enjoy the riding and acclimatize to the high altitudes.

The mountain town of Manali is a melting pot of Indian honeymooners, high-altitude trekkers and high-as-a-kite hippies. Explore the markets, stock up on warm clothes and supplies, then give the bike a check over and fill up the tank before you start out on this epic journey. As you ride out of town, imaginative roads signs ask you to 'Be gentle on my curves' and advise road users, 'Darling I want you but not so fast'. The road instantly starts to climb through stunning Himalayan scenery shrouded by mountain mist. The air gets sharper and thinner, and the backdrop becomes more barren as you approach the Rohtang La pass (3,978 m/13,051 ft), just over an hour's ride from Manali. Early in the season, a wall of snow cleared from the road forms a tunnel through the pass. At Rohtang La, pull over to admire the stupendous view of the summits of Spiti and check your brakes before the road plunges into the Chandra Valley, and the landscape changes to a stark, barren beauty. Tibetan prayer flags appear by the roadside and monasteries beckon from distant mountains as you motor the length of the valley. Top up the tank at the village of Tandi, the only fuel pump on the route, then stay overnight at the nearby town of Keylong either at a guest house or tented camp.

It is a tough ride up and over the 4,892 m (16,049 ft) Baralacha La Pass. Rain can wash away road surfaces, so be prepared to tackle dirt tracks, rocks and boulders and chilly

▽ *The Indus Valley and the Ladakh Range.*

mountain streams on the road ahead. Views of the Himalayas are, at these altitudes, literally breathtaking, so take it slowly as you acclimatize. Spend the night at the tented camp at Sarchu, around 150 km (93 miles) from Keylong, waking refreshed for the next enjoyable section.

The 21 switchbacks of the Gata Loops rise through a lunar landscape in a series of spectacular hairpins towards the Naki La and Lungalacha La passes. Give the engine a rest and cut the switch as you free wheel down from the passes through a wind-eroded landscape. From the military post at Pang, the tarred road rises for around 40 km (25 miles) to the high-altitude Mori Plains. Surrounded by glacial peaks, the area is rich in wildlife including the kyang (wild ass), the red fox and the elusive snow leopard. Only the Tanglang La pass – at 5,325 m (17,470 ft) the world's second highest motorable pass – lies between you and the Indus Valley. The pass affords panoramic views of the Karakoram Mountains before descending in hairpin bends to Miru Gorge. Villages start to appear in patches of green pasture, and monasteries perch on the hillsides adding colour. Ride into Ladkah's capital Leh, having completed one of the world's classic rides. Situated at 3,505 m (11,500 ft), Leh sprawls at the foot of a ruined Tibetan-style palace. Relax for a few days in this beautiful city, as the highest motorable pass is still to come.

The Khardung La is the gateway to the lush, green Nubra Valley. The pass is situated about 37 km (23 miles) by road from Leh. The first 24 km (15 miles), as far as the first checkpoint, are paved. From there the road is mainly loose rock, dirt and occasional snowmelt. This superb feat of engineering winds to an incredible 5,605 m (18,389 ft). The views from the pass to the mountains of Tibet, the Karakoram Range and the Indus Valley are awe-inspiring, and your sense of achievement as you stand next to your bike will be immense.

BIKE: It is possible to take your own bike into India. Bike hire or buy back schemes are available in Delhi or Manali. There are operators offering bike-inclusive tours.

WEATHER WATCH: The road is only open from July to early October.

EXTENDING THE RIDE: From Manali it is around 600 km (373 miles) to Delhi for the start of a ride around Rajasthan.

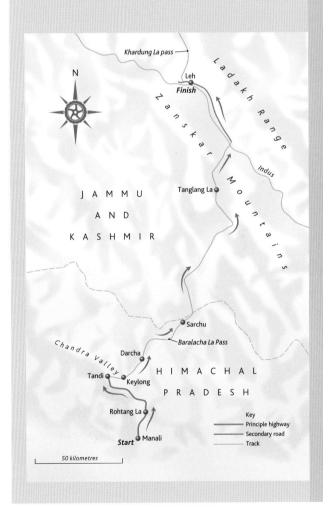

Kathmandu to Lhasa

*Ride from Kathmandu to Lhasa along the 1,000 km (620 mile) 'Friendship Highway',
crossing 5,000 m (16,400 ft) passes and a wild, remote landscape.*

▽ *Kathmandu Valley, in the
Kingdom of Nepal.*

Ride across the roof of the world from the lush tropical valleys of Nepal, through the mountain passes of the Himalayas to the stark, spectacular Tibetan Plateau and the Forbidden City of Lhasa. Held at bay by the Himalayas, for centuries empires longed to be the first to enter the mysterious city of Lhasa. Today it is possible to enter Lhasa on the Friendship Highway, which links these two ancient Buddhist kingdoms.

△ ABOVE LEFT *A Nepalese stupa – a Buddhist mound-like structure.*

△ ABOVE RIGHT *Divine intervention!*

This is one of the world's most spectacular and adventurous road journeys. Altitude sickness, Chinese bureaucracy and corrugated, dusty dirt roads conspire with an inhospitable landscape, making this a tough ride for you and your motorcycle. Navigating the narrow, mountainous roads is a challenging experience, and unpredictable weather can change road surfaces in a few hours. The Chinese have started to black top this route, therefore road works are ongoing and, with landslides a frequent occurrence, roads are often closed and diversions have to be made. The rewards are ancient cities and temples, friendly people, high-altitude desert and stupendous views of the Himalayas, and all this from the seat of your motorcycle.

The Route

Plan on a week to ride to Lhasa. This gives you time to acclimatize, allow for delays but, most of all, time to appreciate this once-in-a-lifetime journey.

Kathmandu's medieval cobbled streets are crowded with holy men, pilgrims and palaces, and the heady smell of incense pervades the air. Test your riding skills as you vie for road space with rickshaw drivers and holy cows, then head east for around 120 km (75 miles) into the Kathmandu Valley and on to the Arniko Highway, Nepal's overland link with China and Tibet. Chinese Customs await at Khasa Gate. From here the road climbs steadily from a lush jungle terrain into the upper valleys of the Himalayas and the desolate desert scenery

tool box

BIKE: Getting your own bike into Tibet is almost impossible and currently there are no options to hire. There are tour operators offering bike-inclusive trips.

WEATHER WATCH: From March to October the weather is generally dry and clear.

EXTENDING THE RIDE: Travel from Kathmandu to Delhi where you can pick up a bike and ride to Rajasthan and Ladakh.

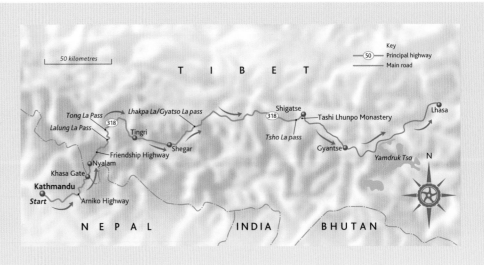

of Tibet. Basic accommodation is available along the route. If it is late in the day when you clear customs, then spend your first night at a guest house in the village of Nyalam, just 30 km (19 miles) from Khasa Gate.

The next day, power over the double passes of Lalung La and Tong La, the first of the 5,000-m (16,400-ft) passes you must cross. Stop and look back at the road you have just ridden, slicing through the gorge between the snow-capped peaks of the main Himalayan range. These incredible views will stay with you throughout the hard ride. When the road is little more than potholes and gravel, and the thin air slows your pace, just turn off the engine, dismount for a few moments and savour the surrounding panorama – you are riding on top of the world! The village of Tingri sits under towering icefields and the superb views are a just reward for a long 150 km (93 mile) stint in the saddle.

Rise early for the 62 km (38 mile) challenging ride along a high-altitude road to the town of Shegar. From Shegar a long, dusty 240 km (149 mile) ride takes you over the highest pass on this route – Lhakpa La/Gyatso La at 5,220 m (17,125 ft) – followed by Tsho La, and through tiny rural villages to Shigatse, and the gold-topped Tashi Lhunpo monastery.

From Shigatse take the southern route via Gyantse. This route is rougher and longer than the northern route, but the views are stupendous. The riding is spectacular as you motor over Karo La Pass, followed by stunning, up-close views of Yamdruk Tso ('turquoise') lake. The road follows the shoreline for quite a distance before making a sudden steep ascent and continuing up over the last pass, Kamba La, descending gently into the green Brahmaputra Valley, filled with orchards and fields irrigated by the Kyichu River. Feast your eyes on the Potala Palace as you follow the road leading into the fabled city of Lhasa, the religious and cultural centre of Tibet.

◁ Potala Palace, Lhasa.

▽ Winding roads in Tibet.

Chiang Mai to Golden Triangle Loop

Ride the Mae Hong Son Loop, head north to the Golden Triangle and return to Chiang Mai via remote eastern provinces.

△ *Taking a break on the Mae Hong Son Loop.*

Sleepy roads wind through mist-shrouded rainforest, weave through lush tropical jungle and trundle through tranquil villages. This is a country renowned for its outstanding natural beauty, distinctive culture and beautiful smiles. The towns and villages strung along the Mekong River and the Burmese (Myanmar) and Laos borders are home to Thailand's colourful hill-tribe people. Mountain trails abound, leading to mystical temples, golden Buddhas and the ruins of ancient cities.

Riding in northern Thailand is relatively undemanding, entertaining and great fun. Rural roads meander past paddy fields, over forested mountain passes and along tropical jungle trails. The distances are short and roads generally quiet. Open-air restaurants serve culinary delights, and are very much part of the Thai road trip, as are the beautiful and inexpensive lodges. For those wanting to up the pace a little, river crossings, log bridges, ruts and slippery slopes offer exciting off-road possibilities. Northern Thailand's network of roads and off-road trails, combined with fantastic food and accommodation, make for a wonderful introduction to riding in Asia.

The Route

The following circuit will take you approximately two weeks if combined with sightseeing and a few days of trekking.

The Mae Hong Son Loop is a network of on- and off-road trails southwest and northwest of the city of Chiang Mai. Roads run through a wild hill country of tropical and teak forests, rugged limestone karsts and densely forested slopes. The region is one of the most mountainous in Thailand and subsequently roads are narrow and winding, consisting of numerous switchbacks and hairpins.

From Chiang Mai head southwest to Mae Chaem for the start of a great ride of thrilling switchbacks to the summit of Doi Inthanon, Thailand's highest peak. Then ride north via mountain passes and thick jungle to the town of Mae Hong Son, located in a valley ringed by forested mountains. From Mae Hong Son the 120 km (75 mile) loop to Pai winds through an area of forests, mountains and limestone caves, offering truly fabulous riding. Pai and nearby Chiang Dao are both major trekking centres, if you want to stretch your legs.

Continue north to Tha Ton, a 115 km (71 mile) ride from Chiang Dao. You are now entering the Golden Triangle, the meeting point of Thailand, Burma (Myanmar) and Laos. This area was once synonymous with opium growing and drug smuggling and, although those days are long gone, the network of roads and trails leading to border towns and

▽ *The picturesque town of Mae Hong Son.*

BIKE: It is possible to take your own bike into Thailand. Bike hire is available in Chiang Mai and Bangkok. There are operators offering bike-inclusive tours both on and off-road, including off-road introductory courses.

WEATHER WATCH: From November to early February it is cool and dry with clear blue skies.

EXTENDING THE RIDE: There is no overland connection to other featured journeys.

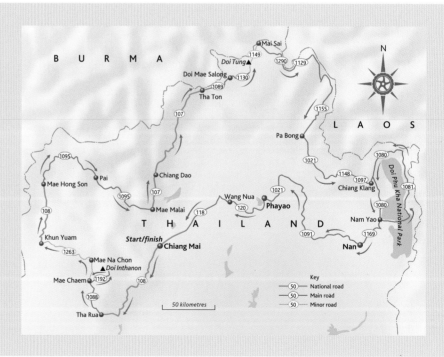

remote villages still exists. This is paradise for motorcyclists seeking to combine riding with visits to colourful hill-tribe villages. The 50 km (31 mile) paved mountain road to Doi Mae Salong takes in beautiful mountain scenery and villages. Continuing out of the village the road snakes through monsoon forest, winding its way up to the 1,800 m (5,900 ft) peak of Doi Tung, where views from the summit are stunning. A short 35 km (22 mile) ride leads to Mai Sai, Thailand's northernmost town, connected to the Burmese (Myanmar) border via a bridge over the Sai River.

After an overnight stay, head southeast riding the deserted rural roads that skirt the border with Laos. The lack of traffic and good tarmac make this region a motorcyclist's favourite. Ride the famous Doi Phu Kha Loops, adventurous mountain roads in and around the beautiful and secluded Doi Phu Kha National Park. Then follow an elevated, twisting road with fabulous views to the 13th century Kingdom of Nan. From Nan it is around 300 km (186 miles) to Chiang Mai via rural Phayao Province. The city of Phayao lies beside a beautiful lake, and the ride west to Wang Nua through magnificent forest affords great views back to it. From Chiang Mai, if you have the time, head south to Thailand's idyllic beaches. Relax under a palm and relive those heady, sweeping trails through the tropical north.

◁ *The Golden Triangle, where Thailand, Burma and Laos meet.*

▽ *Remote villages abound in the Golden Triangle and are well worth exploring.*

A Circuit North from Hanoi

Ride northwest via hill-tribe mountain villages to the hill station of Sa Pa, then north to the remote province of Ha Giang, skirting the Chinese border before returning south to Hanoi.

Ride along mountain roads through mist-shrouded valleys of lush vegetation and steamy bamboo forests. Stay in isolated villages populated by colourful mountain tribes, whose culture has been preserved for centuries. The lively markets in this region attract people from their remote mountain villages to trade goods and socialize, providing an opportunity for young men and women to meet, and they are often referred to as 'love markets'. You will also have the opportunity to trek in the mountains and sample the delicious cuisine, a wonderful combination of French, Thai and Chinese influences.

▽ *Ha Giang, Vietnam.*

The road network is limited, with major highways often little more than single tracks. This is not a full-throttle ride, but an adventure along remote roads that are rarely maintained and can throw up loose gravel, potholes and even river crossings. King of the road is the Belarusian Minsk 125cc. Affectionately known as *con trau gia* ('old buffalo') by the Vietnamese, this robust little bike even has its own fan club. All mechanics know how to fix them and spare parts are readily available, making it the ideal bike for any trip into the mountainous north.

△ ABOVE LEFT *Riding to Dong Van in the Ha Giang Province.*

△ ABOVE RIGHT *Big smiles on the Pha Din Pass.*

The Route

The following 2,100 km (1,305 mile) circuit will take you roughly two weeks if combined with sightseeing and a few days' trekking.

Hanoi's traffic is frenetic, especially in the heat of the day when the smell of two-stroke engines fills the muggy air. Get on the road early and you will be breakfasting below purple mountains before motorcycle mayhem hits the city. NH6 is the main road northwest. It is a busy highway, so allow plenty of time for the 135 km (84 mile) ride to the Mai Chau Valley. If you prefer, take the secondary roads running parallel that lead through beautiful Muong and White Thai villages. Spend the night in the Mai Chau Valley in a stilted guesthouse, your trusty steed parked safely below with the chickens.

The next day, continue heading northwest for around 200 km (124 miles) on a road that climbs steadily, sweeping past tea and coffee plantations, through valleys and over Chen Pass to the town of Son La, which houses the former French prison and museum. Spend the night here, rising early to visit the Black Thai morning market at Thuan Chau before riding over beautiful mountain passes including Pha Din ('Heaven and Earth'), one of the highest in the north. Stop for lunch at the town of Tuan Giao before you tackle the rough and rocky 150 km (93 mile) road to the mountain town of Sin Ho. The scenery is unbelievably beautiful as you traverse passes that cut though steep mountains. Stay overnight in Sin Ho, where the market is a colourful and lively experience. The riding is easier as you leave Sin Ho and descend into the valley, then climb over Tram Ton pass to Sa Pa, at 1,600 m (5,249 ft) a popular hill resort boasting a wide range of accommodation, restaurants and trekking options.

From Sa Pa it is a three-hour ride along Route 70 followed by a 40 km (25 mile) dirt road to the market town of Bac Ha, frequented by the striking Flower Hmong women. From here, a further 40 km (25 miles) along a rocky dirt road will bring you to Xin Man. Stay to catch the Sunday market, which attracts villagers from all over the region, emerging from their remote mountain homes. Visit the market early, leaving plenty of time for the twisting, four-hour journey over mountain passes to Ha Giang, the capital of this remote northern province. From here it is a challenging ride that will test your skills, and your trusty Minsk, as you tackle roads that are often in very poor condition. A guide and permit are obligatory for this section, but the former will provide you with a valuable insight into the region's history and culture, taking you to villages that would otherwise prove difficult to find. You will be rewarded with incredible views from the seat of your 'old buffalo' as clouds lift to reveal colourful villages hidden amongst craggy mountains, and limestone pinnacles that tower above the tiny mountain roads.

The 175 km (109 mile) journey to Meo Vac skirts the Chinese border through a wild, rugged landscape, on roads that see very little traffic. Climb over the 1,500 m (4,921 ft) Ma Pi Leng Pass on a road that twists up the side of an enormous canyon. Meo Vac is lodged in a valley surrounded by vast limestone mountain ranges and perpendicular walls of rock. Spend the night in Meo Vac, ready for the difficult and challenging 230 km (143 mile) ride to Ba Be National Park. Your guide is invaluable for this section of the route, as you traverse forest paths, mountain passes and tackle river crossings. Arriving at Ba Be National Park, the sense of achievement is immense. Relax for a few days, canoe on Ho Ba Be Lake and dine on fresh river fish.

Remounting your Minsk, take the Colie Pass road to Cao Bang, avoiding the National Highway. The 180 km (112 mile) journey is rough, but the scenery is unbelievably beautiful as you ride through dense, ancient forest. Stop for lunch in Cao Bang, then head out in the direction of Ma Phuc Pass to an area of limestone karsts and the villages of the Nung and Tay people. Stay in one of the peaceful villages and explore the region's spectacular scenery. The Ban Gioc waterfalls form a natural border between Vietnam and China, and it is possible to take a day trip on a bamboo raft across to China on the opposite river bank.

For a scenic return to Hanoi, ride south to the border town of Ta Lung then over mountains and through the Dong Khe Valley to the town of Bac Son. It is a bumpy road which turns to dirt for the last 40 km (25 miles), but it winds through beautiful countryside. Stay overnight in Bac Son, returning to Hanoi the next day, an easy 160 km (99 mile) ride. Wash the dirt from your trusty Minsk, its title of 'old buffalo' well earned.

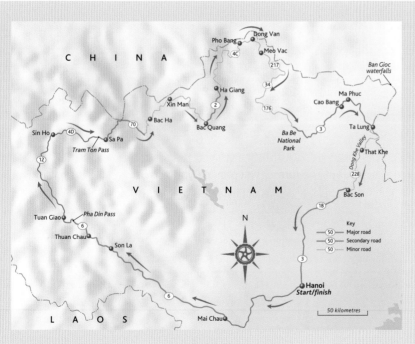

BIKE: It is now possible to take your own bike into Vietnam. Hire a Minsk in Hanoi. There are operators offering bike-inclusive trips.

WEATHER WATCH: The dry season runs from October to April. Avoid the rainy season during May to September when dirt roads turn to mud.

EXTENDING THE RIDE: No overland connection to other featured journeys.

The Northern Silk Road: Xian to Urumqi

The Northern Silk Road skirts the edge of the Gobi Desert, runs through the infamous Hexi (Gansu) Corridor, visits the last outpost of the Chinese Empire and ends on the shores of Heaven Lake.

The fabled Silk Road opened up the mysteries of the Chinese Empire to the West, and for centuries caravans journeyed from the imperial capital at Xian across inhospitable deserts and over desolate mountain passes to trade with merchants from India, Persia and the Mediterranean. Centuries on and China still remains a mystery, as decades of restrictions on motorcycle travel have hindered the adventure of following the route of these intrepid travellers. As China becomes more accessible, it is now possible to join fellow motorcyclists and ride sections of this remote route on bikes that, like the camels before them, are built to withstand the harsh and unforgiving terrain.

Whilst the riding is not too difficult, the journey can be challenging, due mainly to frustrating regulations and frequently dramatic weather changes. Pack your waterproofs and some warm layers, but don't forget your shades and some lightweight gear for those days when the temperature rises above 40°C (104°F). The surfaces on the major roads are generally good, but there is a constant rebuilding and restructuring programme and, as you approach road works, you may well be waved off onto a side road where the road condition quickly deteriorates. There may be stretches of dirt and gravel and sometimes sand. Riding in China is ultimately rewarding, however, as you ride along roads little-travelled by modern motorcycles. Big bikes are a rarity, so expect an excited and enthusiastic gathering wherever you stop!

The Route

Allow two weeks to complete this epic 3,500 km (1,864 mile) journey.

The imperial capital Xian was, for the caravans, either the start or the finish of an arduous journey. Ride out of the ancient city walls heading west towards the sands of the great Gobi Desert. A 700 km (435 mile) ride takes you to the border of Gansu province, a wild and rugged land. Enter the mouth of the infamous Hexi (Gansu) Corridor at the city of Lanzhou. Once a major transport hub along the Silk Road, these days the city is famed for

▽ *The imperial city of Xian.*

its delicious beef noodles. Stay overnight in one of the government-owned hotels you will find along this route.

△ *The Great Wall of China is an extraordinary sight.*

From Lanzhou it is around a 300 km (186 mile) ride to the town of Wuwei at the eastern end of the Hexi (Gansu) Corridor, a 1,000 km (621 mile) route which winds between the stunning snow-capped mountains of the Qilian Shan in the south and the vast expanse of the Gobi to the north, narrowing to as little as 15 km (9 miles) in parts. The ride through this region is spectacular.

Leaving Wuwei there are fantastic views of the Great Wall as you ride the 500 km (311 miles) to Jiayuguan along roads that are, generally, in reasonable condition. The magnificent restored fortress at Jiayuguan lies on the Jiayuguan Pass and is beautifully framed by the stark, snow-capped Qilian Mountains. The fortress controlled the pass and marked the edge of the Chinese Empire and the end of the Great Wall. Beyond the fortress lay hostile tribes, extremes of weather and the constantly shifting desert sands.

Road conditions on the 400 km (249 mile) stretch to Dunhuang can be difficult if road works force you onto the gravel roads. Perched on the edge of the desert, Dunhuang was an important oasis town providing shelter from the extremes of weather. It also served as a centre for culture and religious art, as tradesmen exchanged ideas in addition to their financial negotiations. The Buddhist caves at Mogao, just 25 km (16 miles) south of Dunhuang, were the first Buddhist temples to be reached on journeying into the Chinese Empire and are now a UNESCO World Heritage Site.

The roads through the Gobi Desert have long stretches of straight road with little traffic, so you can get some speed up as you ride the 440 km (273 miles) to the town of Hami, within the province of Xinjiang, a vast region covered by deserts and mountains. The Tian Shan ('Heavenly Mountains') run from west to east, and to the south is the Taklamakan

BIKE: Current restrictions mean it is very difficult and expensive to take your own bike in to China. Bike hire is not currently an option, but there are operators offering bike-inclusive tours.

WEATHER WATCH: April to October is the only time this route is passable.

EXTENDING THE RIDE: There is no overland connection to other featured journeys, but a short flight will take you to Ulaanbaatar where you can pick up a tour in Mongolia.

Desert, one of the most inhospitable deserts on earth. The terrain is harsh with little water, so quench your thirst at Hami, famous for its mouth-watering melons, and pack a couple into your tank bag for the 400 km (249 mile) ride to Turpan. The extremes of weather on this section take their toll on the road surfaces, and the inevitable detours onto gravel or dirt roads can make it a hot, dusty ride. Turpan is located in a depression 80 m (262 ft) below sea level. A major oasis on the Northern Silk Road, its famous vineyards are irrigated by snowmelt from the Tian Shan. Ride 10 km (6 miles) east of Turpan and spend some time in the paradise of Grape Valley. Dine on traditional Uighur fare of roasted lamb kebabs under the welcome shade of the grape trellises, and then take a short ride out to the Flaming Mountains for a spectacular sunset. The red sandstone of the mountains appears to flicker in the desert haze.

Leave the green oasis of Turpan to ride 200 km (124 miles) across the vast plains and through a stark landscape to Urumqi. The road is surrounded on either side by desert, and the Tian Shan provides a stunning backdrop. Temperatures can top 40°C (104°F), but it is a dry heat with high winds. Urumqi is the end of the Chinese section of the Silk Road. Celebrate the conclusion of your journey at Heaven Lake, 110 km (68 miles) east of Urumqi. The turquoise lake is perched at a cool 2,000 m (6,561ft) and surrounded by snow-covered mountains and pine forest. The cool air is refreshing and walking trails take you through forests and flower-filled meadows. Spend the night in a traditional Kazak yurt by the lakeside, gazing at the stars whilst you relive your journey along one of the world's most famous trading routes.

◁ *The Flaming Mountains are stunning at sunset.*

▽ *Yurts, camels and some less-traditional transport at Heaven Lake.*

Ulaanbaatar to Gobi Desert Loop

Ride a loop from Ulaanbaatar south through the Gobi Desert to a region where dinosaurs roamed and great empires flourished, returning to Ulaanbaatar via the Khogno Khan mountains.

Imagine riding under the widest blue sky you have ever seen with only camels, sheep and horsemen sharing the road. The sense of space and freedom as you ride across the open steppe of Mongolia is simply breathtaking. Mongolia's beauty lies in its natural wonders and hospitable people. Teenage horsemen ride like the wind, birds of prey circle the skies and scattered across the steppe are the traditional *gers* (tents) of the Mongolian people. This vast land is one of the least populated countries on earth, and the nomadic Mongolians live a life

▽*A traditional Mongolian ger camp.*

little-changed since the days of Genghis Khan, travelling by horse and living off the land. Tourist *ger* camps providing comfortable traditional accommodation are scattered across the country, making it possible to experience this most traditional way of life every night of your trip.

Mongolia is hard to beat when it comes to the variety of riding terrain. Ride through grassland, across desert and over mountain passes. Potholed roads give way to stony tracks, whilst riding in the Gobi alternates between grey gravel and sections of deep sand. Petrol stations, as we know them, do not exist, and a GPS is a welcome piece of technology in a country with so few roads. With only a handful of tarmac roads, rough tracks and horse trails connect most of this unspoiled wilderness, making it the perfect off-road motorcycling destination. If you enjoy the challenge of riding across unfamiliar terrain, spending your nights camping under a vast star-scattered sky, then Mongolia is pure motorcycle heaven.

The Route

Allow a week to ten days for the following circular route, which provides a taste of adventurous riding across mountain, desert and steppe.

Arrive into the capital Ulaanbaatar in early July and you will witness Mongolia's famous Nadaam festival. Test your skills in the *eriin gurvan naadam* ('three manly games')

△ ABOVE LEFT *The archery competition, part of the Nadaam festival.*

△ ABOVE RIGHT *Horse racing at Nadaam, another of the 'three manly games'.*

△ ABOVE LEFT *The Gobi Desert.*

△ ABOVE RIGHT *Sometimes you need a helping hand.*

OVERLEAF *Racing in the Finke Desert.*

of archery, wrestling, and horse racing. There is music and dancing and the Genghis Khan vodka flows. Leave the festivities behind and head south into the steppe for around 250 km (155 miles) on one of the few main roads. The tarmac eventually disappears, but this is where the adventure begins as you discover for yourself the magic of this beautiful country. The final section of the day's ride is across rough dirt tracks to the spectacular granite rock formations of Baga Gazriin Chuluu, rising 1,768 m (5,800 ft) above sea level.

Relax for the evening at a nearby *ger* camp, rising early the next morning for the long, 400 km (248 mile) ride south into the Gobi Desert to the town of Dalandzadgad. Find a base for a few days in the region west of the town and explore the area, riding along stony desert tracks and testing your skills in the sandy terrain. Ride out to Bayandzag ('Flaming Cliffs'), where dinosaur eggs were discovered in the 1920s; visit the 'glacier' canyon of Yolim Am ('Eagle's Mouth'); and strike out to the immense Khongor Els, Mongolia's largest sand dunes.

Head north again, across the vast plains to the Ogniyn monastery, spending the night at another *ger* camp by the Ogni River. From Ogniyn it is a 250 km (155 mile) ride to the

BIKE: It is now possible to take your own bike into Mongolia. Alternatively join an operator-run tour.

WEATHER WATCH: July to September is really the only time to ride this route by motorcycle.

EXTENDING THE RIDE: There is no overland connection to other featured journeys, but a short flight will take you to Beijing where you can pick up a tour along the Northern Silk Road.

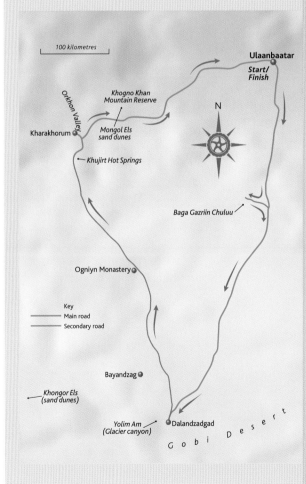

Orkhon Valley and the ruined city of Kharakhorum, Mongolia's ancient capital. Its walls surround the exquisite Buddhist monastery of Erdene Zuu, once more an active monastery. If the riding has been a little tough, take a soak at the nearby Khujirt hot springs and relax overnight at a *ger* camp.

From here the 100 km (62 mile) ride northeast to the Khogno Khan Mountain Reserve takes you over rocky mountains, across steppe and through dense forest. Spend the night at a camp close to the Mongol Els sand dunes, before rejoining the tarmac for the final 300 km (186 mile) ride back to Ulaanbaatar. 'The Land of Blue Skies' will leave a huge impression on you and is a truly magnificent motorcycling destination.

AUSTRALASIA

Darwin to Alice Springs: the Top End to the Red Centre

Ride from Darwin and the lush tropical landscape of the Top End through the arid deserts of the Northern Territory, across the Tropic of Capricorn to Australia's Red Centre.

This region of Australia is home to the Aboriginal people and the journey starts and ends at two of their most sacred sites. Kakadu, in Australia's Northern Territory, sits at the tip of the tropical north. The park is a breathtakingly beautiful wilderness area and a walk amongst craggy escarpments reveals thousands of Aboriginal rock paintings. The lush tropical setting of the Top End is replaced by a barren, arid landscape as you ride south through the heart of the Northern Territory, where outback tracks branch off from the tarmac into the desert and remote roadhouses survive on the trade of passing vehicles.

▽ *The road to Uluru.*

△ ABOVE LEFT *Stopping to admire Uluru at sunset.*

△ ABOVE RIGHT *Darwin, where this journey begins.*

As you approach the deserts of the Red Centre, strange, surreal formations appear against the vast blue skies and the earth turns red. Here are some of Australia's most amazing natural wonders, none more so than Uluru which rises dramatically from Aboriginal ancestral lands, changing colour throughout the day and enchanting visitors from across the globe. A journey through this region gives you a momentary taste of life in the outback and a snapshot of the history of this ancient land and its people.

This is a long ride from the tip of Australia's Northern Territory to its Red Centre. The Stuart Highway, often referred to as 'The Track', is named after John McDouall Stuart, the first European to cross Australia from south to north. It bisects the heart of Australia, and riding this road gives you a real appreciation for the scale of this huge country. Fully sealed in the mid-eighties, its entire length passes through remote outback Australia with services and fuel stops well signposted. You can ride for hours without seeing another vehicle, along a road that stretches far into the horizon. However, this journey is not about the road. It is about the places you visit and characters you meet at the roadhouses and towns along the way, as you experience the hospitality and humour of the people who make their home in this harsh environment.

BIKE: It is possible to take your own bike into Australia. Bike hire is available in Darwin and Alice Springs. There are operators offering bike-inclusive tours.

WEATHER WATCH: The best months for the tropical north are May to October. The Red Centre is best visited October to November and March to May.

EXTENDING THE RIDE: Around 400 km (249 miles) south of Alice Springs is the turnoff to the Oodnadatta Track at Marla, or continue south for 155 km (96 miles) and join the track from Coober Pedy.

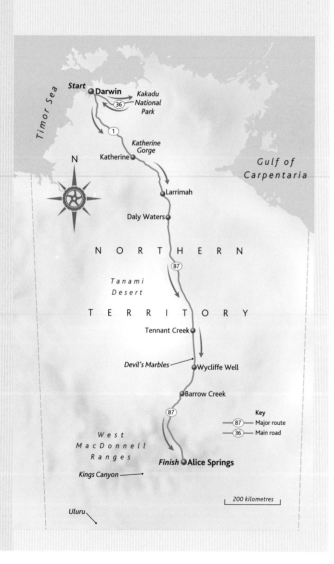

The Route

The Stuart Highway covers approximately 2,800 km (1,770 miles) from Darwin to Adelaide. The following route covers the 1,500 km (932 mile) section from Darwin to Alice Springs. The road can be ridden in a few days, but with visits to the national parks at either end, allow at least ten days to two weeks.

Leave Darwin on the Stuart Highway but branch off east after around 45 km (28 miles) onto the Arnhem Highway for the 150 km (93 mile) ride to Kakadu National Park. It is well worth the detour for a few days to experience the incredible diversity of vegetation and animal life that thrives in the park.

Return to The Track, riding south for around 300 km (186 miles) to the town of Katherine, jumping-off point for visits to the magnificent Katherine Gorge. From Katherine it is a long, hot and dusty 1,100 km (683 mile) ride to Alice Springs. The highlights of this section of the journey are the bush pubs along the route that provide accommodation, fuel and entertainment to passing travellers. The Larrimah Hotel, 175 km (109 miles) south of Katherine, is a typical outback pub that boasts the highest bar in the Northern Territory. A further 100 km (62 miles) down The Track is the historic Daly Waters Pub, which has held a licence since 1893. The walls are lined with visitor memorabilia, and it makes a good overnight stop to share a few beers with fellow travellers and fuel up for the approach to the deserts of central Australia.

The landscape becomes more stark and sparse as you blast down The Track for 400 km (249 miles) to Tennant Creek. There is a tale that the town was settled when a wagonload of beer broke down in the 1930s and the drivers decided to make themselves a home whilst they sampled the goods. As you leave Tennant Creek the scenery starts to blend to a rugged, desert landscape. A 100 km (62 mile) ride brings you to the Devil's Marbles, or Karlu Karlu – huge rounded boulders thought by local Aborigines to be the eggs of the Rainbow Serpent. It is worth camping in the area to experience sunrise and sunset when the Marbles and the surrounding desert landscape are truly spectacular. If you prefer a little more comfort and the chance to see an extra-terrestrial, a short 25 km (16 mile) ride south brings you to Wycliffe Well, renowned for its UFO sightings and its vast range of beers! A short distance south, the Barrow Creek pub is one of the oldest roadhouses on The Track. Originally a telegraph station, it has a bloody history and is well worth a stop before the final 282 km (175 mile) push to Alice Springs.

Pass the turnoff for outback tracks that lead east to Queensland and west through the Tanami Desert before rolling into Alice Springs, 'capital' of the Red Centre. It is a fun outback town surrounded by the orange and purple glow of the MacDonnell Ranges. From Alice Springs there is a fantastic route along a combination of paved and dirt tracks out to the West MacDonnell Ranges, across to Kings Canyon via the 200 km (124 mile) Mereenie Loop, then southwest for around 320 km (199 miles) along a paved road to Uluru, which rises spectacularly from the surrounding plain.

▽ BELOW LEFT *Dirt roads near Alice Springs.*

▽ BELOW RIGHT *The dusty roads of the Red Centre.*

The Oodnadatta Track

Take a ride through desert plains along the famous Oodnadatta Track in south Australia. Ride from Marree to Oodnadatta, then across to the opal mining town of Coober Pedy.

△ *Keep an eye out for Australia's unusual wildlife.*

South Australia's outback is easily accessible from Adelaide, but once out there it is hot, wild and desolate. It's a region renowned for its larger-than-life characters, whose tall stories and humour add colour to the desolate landscape. The Oodnadatta Track follows the route of the old Ghan Railway, named after the Afghan camel trails that trekked the route prior to the advent of the railway. The journey is one of discovery, the region's history unfolding along the route. End your journey in Coober Pedy, which retains the air of a frontier town, its inhabitants still mining for that perfect opal.

Ride one of Australia's legendary desert tracks, encountering punishing corrugations, rocky tracks and suicidal wildlife, especially around dusk. You will also encounter bull dust, a fine powder dust that can cover deep holes and look like smooth track. Once you've picked your bike up a few times you start to spot the signs – dual sports and enduros are more suited to this terrain. The condition of the track will depend on recent weather conditions, so check the weather forecast before setting out and pre-plan fuel and water stops. This is an outback track that is generally well-maintained and regularly used, but don't underestimate the possible dangers. It is wild and remote and the riding can be extremely challenging, but no trip to Australia is complete without a ride through the outback. With a little pre-planning, it will be the highlight of your visit.

The Route

Allowing for a couple of overnight stops in the outback, this route should take you three days.

The Oodnadatta Track begins at the old railhead of Marree. Ride out of town in the early morning light, while the air is still cool, and get onto the track. Concentration is key, as you scan the road for the best line to take. If you've not ridden one of the desert pistes before, take your time while you get a feel for the terrain. Around 100 km (62 miles) out of Marree the illusion of a vast ocean shimmers on the horizon. As the mirage comes into focus, the ocean becomes the white salt crust of Lake Eyre South. Once past the salt lake look out for a turn-off about 25 km (16 miles) further down the track. If you want to camp out under the vast outback skies there is a campsite at Coward Springs. If you prefer a bed, William Creek lies a further 75 km (47 miles) down the Oodnadatta Track. This small town is surrounded by the world's largest cattle station. Fuel, food and accommodation are available at the famous William Creek Hotel, built in 1887 to service the Ghan Railway.

After William Creek the track is rougher and stonier. The next 200 km (124 miles) will take you to the town of Oodnadatta, which served as a railhead until 1929. The vision of

▽ *Riding the Oodnadatta Track is one of the ultimate Australian experiences.*

△ ABOVE LEFT *Coober Pedy, the famous opal-mining town.*

△ ABOVE RIGHT *A welcome sight after a dusty ride.*

the Pink Roadhouse is a fabulous sight after your ride through the desert. In addition to brightening up the landscape, the roadhouse provides accommodation, the legendary 'oodnaburger' and good advice about the roads ahead. Stock up with fuel and provisions, give the bike a good check over then head back out into the desert.

The current track finishes at Marla, 200 km (124 miles) further west and out on the Stuart Highway. Alternatively head southwest for 230 km (143 miles) across the Painted Desert to Coober Pedy, a wild opal-mining town. The road to Coober Pedy varies from wide and gravely to stony, with plenty of hidden bull dust. It can be ridden in a day, but there is camping around 135 km (84 miles) from Coober Pedy. The scenery on this route is awe-inspiring and the light is magical, particularly at dawn and dusk. The *Mad Max* movies were filmed in this area, taking advantage of the vast open spaces and the lunar-like landscape. At Coober Pedy wash off the dust at an underground hotel and join the town's residents and visitors for a well-earned beer in one of the lively bars.

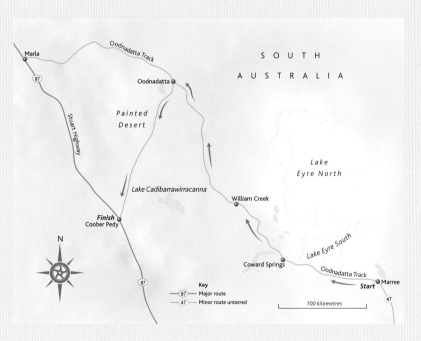

BIKE: It is possible to take your own bike into Australia. Bike hire is available in Melbourne and Adelaide. There are operators offering bike-inclusive tours.

WEATHER WATCH: May to September is the best time to visit. October to March is not recommended due to high temperatures.

EXTENDING THE RIDE: Join the Stuart Highway at either Marla or Coober Pedy and head either north to Alice Springs or south to Adelaide for routes through the Red Centre or the Great Ocean Road.

127

The Great Ocean Road

Ride the Great Ocean Road which runs west along Victoria's coast for 285 km (177 miles) from Torquay to Warrnambool.

The state of Victoria lies on Australia's southwest coast. For a small state it packs in a lot of sights, many within reach of a long day's ride out of Melbourne. Visit the spectacular rocky outcrops of the Grampians National Park, the snow-covered Victorian Alps or the beautiful wine regions of the Yarra Valley. A highlight of any trip to this region is a ride along the Great Ocean Road. The road was blasted from the rocky cliffs along Victoria's rugged southwest coast by more than 3,000 returned soldiers in honour of their fallen comrades in the First World War. It winds through rainforest and past some of the best surfing beaches in Australia, following a jagged coastline where the powerful Southern Ocean smashes against the rocky headlands.

▽ *The coastal road through the Otway Range.*

This is a leisurely and scenic ride on good tarmac, giving you time to admire the outstanding views and visit places of interest along the way. The road hugs the coast between Torquay and Apollo Bay. From Apollo Bay the road heads inland through Otway National Park, rejoining the coast at Port Campbell National Park. The ride from Moonlight Head, the 'Shipwreck Coast', is the most spectacular, with sandstone cliffs dropping away into the ocean and unusual rock formations rising from the ocean. The coastline can be wild and windy even during the summer months, so keep your windproof jacket on.

△ *Otway National Park has a great treetop walk if you want a break from the bike.*

The Route

The Great Ocean Road can easily be ridden in a day, but take a few days and explore the wild coast, lively resort towns and beautiful national parks that line the route.

From Melbourne, it is a 95 km (60 mile) ride southwest to Torquay and the start of the Great Ocean Road. Lively Torquay is at the centre of Victoria's 'surf coast' and the town buzzes during the surf season. The road continues through the town of Anglesea and on to the popular resort of Lorne. There is a great choice of accommodation and restaurants and a regular

BIKE: It is possible to take your own bike into Australia. Bike hire is available in Melbourne. There are operators offering bike-inclusive tours.

WEATHER WATCH: February to April is a good time to visit. The weather is warm and the beaches and towns are less crowded.

EXTENDING THE RIDE: It is a further 650 km (400 mile) ride to Adelaide for routes to the Red Centre and the Oodnadatta Track.

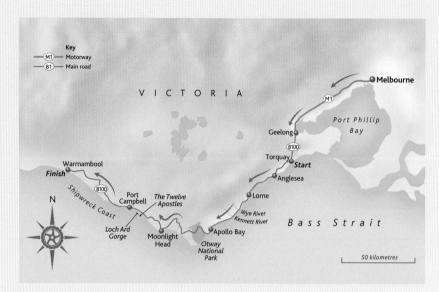

calendar of festivals throughout the year. From Lorne the road snakes along the coastline, descending to the Wye and Kennett Rivers, tranquil spots for camping and bushwalking.

A little further along the coast, Apollo Bay nestles between green hills and wild ocean surf. Popular with artists and musicians, local pubs feature regular music sessions, and good accommodation can be found in the surrounding hills and valleys. From Apollo Bay the Great Ocean Road heads inland through the Otway National Park, curving through rainforest. The final stretch from Moonlight Head is known as the Shipwreck Coast, owing to its reputation for luring victims to its rugged cliffs. For motorcyclists this section of the road is the most fun. Views are fabulous as bends hug the coastline, offering far-reaching views of the Twelve Apostles, limestone pillars towering 65 m (213 ft) out of the ocean. Nearby Loch Ard Gorge was named after a ship, whose only two survivors sheltered in one of the caves. Just west of Port Campbell, the double-arched rock formation of London Bridge comes into view. The last stretch of the road winds through farming country and on to Warrnambool, and the end of the Great Ocean Road.

◁ BELOW LEFT *The Great Ocean Road runs along a beautiful stretch of coast.*

▽ BELOW RIGHT *The Twelve Apostles.*

South Island Circuit

Ride a circuit from Christchurch encompassing much of South Island's varied landscapes and stunning roads.

New Zealand's South Island is wild and spectacular, a land of magnificent natural beauty offering an incredible variety of vast, powerful landscapes. Awesome fjords and glaciers, rainforest, turquoise lakes and ancient, native forests are all enclosed by a wild and rugged coastline.

New Zealand is considered one of the world's top motorcycling destinations. Perfect roads lead over hills and mountains through stunning natural wonders. Roads are generally quiet and often deserted, giving you the feeling of riding through an untouched land. Although New Zealand is a relatively small country you will experience an incredible feeling of space, riding through a landscape that changes from farmland to alpine, then tropical in just a few hours.

▽ *Mount Cook, the highest mountain in New Zealand.*

The Route

△ *A woolly road block.*

Allowing for sightseeing, the following loop should take roughly two weeks.

Start your trip with a ride to Mount Cook, New Zealand's highest peak. Head inland from Christchurch through the heart of gentle countryside. The road rises over Burkes Pass (701 m/2,300 ft), winding to beautiful Lake Tekapo, a turquoise glacial lake framed against a backdrop of snow-capped mountain peaks. Head southwest for about 45 km (28 miles) then take the road to Lake Pukaki for fabulous views to Mount Cook – a fantastic end to your first day's ride. From the lake the road continues for around 60 km (37 miles) to the entrance of the Aoraki/Mount Cook National Park. If you want to explore the vast peaks and glaciers on foot, the nearby town of Twizel makes a good base. From Twizel head east for around 265 km (165 miles) to the coast, following the SH1 south to Dunedin, a city with a very Scottish history. Continue along SH1 to the Southlands region, the southeastern reaches of the island. Motorcycle legend Burt Munro, 'The World's Fastest Indian', was born in Invercargill and much of the film of the same name was shot in the area.

△ *Riding near Milford Sound.*

▷ *The Fox Glacier in the Westland National Park.*

OVERLEAF *Pausing on a dirt track in Iceland.*

Leave the surf of the Pacific, riding inland towards the breathtaking wilderness of Fjordland National Park. The town of Te Anau serves as the main transport and accommodation hub, and the 120 km (75 mile) ride from here to Milford Sound is one of the most spectacular roads you will ever ride. Rise early, top up with fuel and get on the road before the tourist buses. Scenery unfolds past rolling farmland as the road follows Lake Te Anau before entering verdant, dense forests. Ride past Mirror Lake and along the avenue of the Disappearing Mountain, which appears to shrink as you ride towards it. Climb the steep road to Homer Tunnel, a 1,219 m (3,999 ft) tunnel cut from solid rock, emerging between sheer mountain faces into Cheddau Valley. Milford Sound is an amazing 22 km (14 mile) long fjord dominated by the 1,692 m (5,551 ft) Mitre Peak. After your incredible ride, relax and appreciate the scale of this natural wonder on a boat trip into the open sea.

Returning to Te Anau, a further 172 km (108 mile) scenic ride brings you to Queenstown, the world's adrenaline capital. If you have the urge to throw yourself out of a plane or hang from a bungee rope, this is undoubtedly the place to do it. Ride the 100 km (62 mile) to Wanaka over the Crown Range Road, the highest main road in New Zealand at 1,121 m (3,688 ft). The narrow paved road zigzags up the mountain offering stupendous views down to the Arrow Valley, and back to Lake Wakatipu and Queenstown. On the way down, the sight of flimsy, lacy underwear may necessitate an emergency stop as the Bra Fence comes into view!

From Wanaka it is a rollercoaster of a ride to the west coast over the 563 m (1,857 ft) Haast Pass, once used by the Maori in search of greenstone (jade). From Haast a two-hour ride north brings you to the Westland National Park. The colossal sparkling white glaciers of Fox and Franz Josef cut through the rainforest, almost reaching the road.

Continue north to Hokitika. Mid-March sees the town's Wildfoods Festival, where you can sample such delicacies as chocolate worm truffles and deep-fried grasshoppers. From Hokitika the road skirts the coast affording wonderful views. At Greymouth head inland, returning to Christchurch over Arthur's Pass, a spectacular 230 km (143 mile) road cutting through the breathtaking, dramatic scenery of the southern Alps.

BIKE: It is possible to take your own bike into New Zealand. Bike hire is available in Christchurch. There are operators offering bike-inclusive tours.

WEATHER WATCH: October to May is the best time to visit. Winter runs from June to September.

EXTENDING THE RIDE: No overland connection to other featured journeys.

EUROPE

The Ringroad Tour

From Seydisfjördur on the east coast this route runs anti-clockwise around the Ringroad, which circumnavigates the island for 1,339 km (832 miles).

▽ *The landscape in Iceland is elemental and untamed.*

Created by wild natural forces and forged from fire and ice, Iceland is a pure, wild and untamed land of ice caps, fjords and glaciers. Visitors are treated to volcanic eruptions, steam explosions and bubbling mud pools. The country reshapes itself before your eyes, and as you ride around Iceland you will witness the elements in their most raw form and nature at its most powerful.

There is no motorway and the Ringroad, the only main paved road, has stretches of gravel, narrow passes and blind bends, particularly in the remote and desolate northeast. If you have a dual sport bike, there are some fantastic and challenging gravel mountain roads branching from the Ringroad into the wild interior. This is a country forged by the forces of nature and the winds can be ferocious. Motorcycling here provides a real feel of experiencing the elements, not to mention the wildlife – there are more sheep in Iceland than humans and they wander the roads at will.

The Route

A week will allow you to circuit the Ringroad and visit some of the places highlighted here, but if you allow two weeks you will have time to get out on foot or head inland to tackle the gravel tracks and untamed interior.

From Seydisfjördur head inland and west for 208 km (130 miles) through the remote wilderness of the northeast. The area around Lake Myvatn is stunningly beautiful, and it is worth spending a couple of days by the lake exploring the hot springs and lava towers and climbing the Hverfjall volcano. It is also known as 'Midge Lake' so you may want to keep your visor down as you ride the 35 km (22 mile) circuit.

From Lake Myvatn it is just over an hour's ride to Akureyri, Iceland's second largest town lying just 100 km (62 miles) south of the Arctic Circle. Accommodation options are plentiful and there is a lively night life.

Top up with fuel and get an early start, as it is a long 450 km (280 mile) ride west to the tip of the Snaefellsnes Peninsula. The Snaefellsjökull volcano, made world-famous by Jules Verne's *Journey to the Centre of the Earth*, dominates this rugged peninsula. Stay under the shadow of Snaefellsjökull and spend a day relaxing before heading 200 km (125 miles) south to Reykjavik, Iceland's vibrant capital.

From Reykjavik, an hour's ride on Route 36 will take you directly to Pingvellir and the area known as the Golden Circle. Pingvellir, the site of Iceland's democratic assemblies for over 800 years, perches on top of a major fault line. Stay a few days as there is much to explore in this staggeringly beautiful region, including the bubbling hot springs of Geysir, where the erupting Strokkur (Icelandic for 'churn') emits a spectacular 30 m (98 ft) jet of

△ *The Strokkur geyser erupts every five to ten minutes.*

139

△ *Gullfoss, one of the most popular tourist attractions in Iceland.*

water and steam every few minutes. At nearby Gullfoss ('Golden Waterfall'), torrents of water thunder into a huge gorge.

Drop south back onto the Ringroad at Selfoss heading east for 128 km (80 miles) towards Iceland's southernmost point and the black sand beaches at Vik. Your ride will take you past the foot of the Eyjafjallajökull and Myrdalsjökull glaciers; active volcanoes simmer beneath their icy caps. The southeast section of the Ringroad is dominated by Vatnajökull, Europe's largest ice cap. It is immense, awe-inspiring and covers an area of 3,000 sq km (1,864 sq miles), its glacial fingers almost touching the road. Watch icebergs float in the deep Jökulsárlón Glacier Lagoon before leaving the south coast and climbing into the rugged alpine landscape of the eastern fjords. Break your journey with an overnight stay near Höfn.

The final 275 km (171 mile) section of the Ringroad takes you over the Almannaskard Pass into fjord country, where the spectacular road winds through numerous steep-walled inlets, squeezing between mountain and sea as you make your way back to Seydisfjördur.

It is a harsh and sometimes lonely route, yet the scenery is immensely powerful and spectacularly dramatic, and like no other place you will ever ride.

▷ *Jökulsárlón, one of a number of Iceland's glacial lakes.*

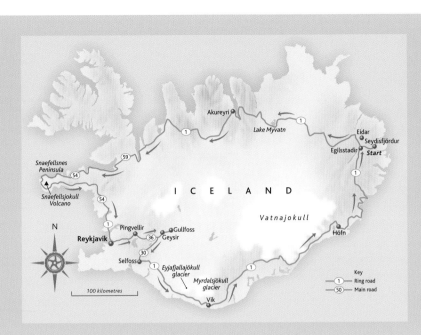

BIKE: It is possible to take your own bike into Iceland. Bike hire is not easily available but there are operators offering bike-inclusive tours.

WEATHER WATCH: May to September is the best time to visit. Mountain roads open from late June. The tourist board hotline provides daily road and weather information.

EXTENDING THE RIDE: Weekly boats depart for Bergen in Norway and Scotland's Shetland Isles.

Stavanger to Andalsnes

This route runs through Norway's magnificent fjordland on the west coast.

The land of the Vikings is not as far away, or as cold, as you may think. The raw power and sheer magnificence of the scenery will take your breath away. Norway's natural beauty is impossible to imagine. The air is clear and the elements are awesome, offering rugged coastline, plunging river valleys and those fabulous fjords. At Norway's northernmost point is Nordkapp ('North Cape'), which lies 400 km (250 miles) deep into the Arctic Circle and is accessible by road through a wild and often inhospitable landscape.

▽ *The fjords of Norway are a spectacular sight.*

△ ABOVE LEFT *Mingling with some very tame locals.*

△ ABOVE RIGHT *Beautiful Bergen is a lovely place to stay.*

Norway offers a unique riding experience. Spectacular serpentine roads wend their way skywards almost, it seems, to Valhalla. Multiple switchbacks and nail-biting narrow roads run alongside fjords, mountains and thundering waterfalls, cutting through rock faces and zigzagging over mountains. It is often impossible to go in a straight line, with some tunnels even turning an incredible 360 degrees. Like waterproofs, ferries are a necessity in this land of water and the ferry journey itself is often an inexpensive means of seeing some of Norway's most impressive and wildest scenery. Bikes are always first on and off, so there is little time wasted and you get to roll off the ferry and hit the tarmac before the hordes. The riding is wildly exhilarating and almost every road will bring a smile to your face – yes they are that good! Best of all, summer offers almost 24-hour daylight – ample time to ride Norway's superb roads.

The Route

The following route should take about a week, but allow a little longer if you want to explore the national parks.

Roll off the ferry at Stavanger and pick up RT13, following it all the way to Odda, a distance of around 270 km (168 miles). The route encompasses short ferry rides, stunning vistas and a couple of nice mountain crossings. Detour onto RT520 between Sand and

△ *The Trollstigen, a rollercoaster of a road.*

Røldal, and ride up through the majestic Ekkjeskaret gorge. West of Røldal, ride the old road across the Seljestadjuvet, where you are rewarded with a magnificent view of the Folgefonn Glacier. This is an incredible introduction to Norway's superb roads and wonderful fjords, and just a taster of the thrilling riding in store.

From Odda, RT550 hugs the west side of the Sørfjorden, one of the three arms of the magnificent Hardangerfjorden. At the pretty village of Utne, take a ferry across to Kvanneid and join RT7, which clings to the north shore of the Hardangerfjorden for just over 100 km (62 miles) into Bergen. Surrounded by mountains, Bergen's cobbled streets are lined with brightly painted hotels, bustling bars and superb restaurants. Bergen is also the gateway to the western fjords.

From Bergen motor east for a couple of hours to Gudvangen, where you pick up the Gudvangen-Lærdal ferry, a 2.5-hour ride out through the Nærlandsfjord, a branch of the Sognefjord, which at 200 km (124 miles) long and 1,300 m (4,265 ft) deep, is the world's longest and deepest fjord. The view from the deck of sheer cliffs and cascading waterfalls is simply breathtaking. Leave the ferry at Kaupanger, and enjoy the short ride west alongside the Sognefjord to Balestrand, a relaxed resort set against a mountain backdrop and a good place to spend the night.

Change down a gear or two now as you head onto the mountain passes. Pick up the RT13 again and start by going across the Gaularfjell mountain on a fabulous narrow, winding road. There's a particularly nice viewpoint some 30 km (18 miles) from Balestrand as you head up, and a couple of lovely waterfalls on the other side as you head towards Moskog. At Moskog, head northeast on the E39 to Stryn, a distance of around 120 km (75 miles). A short detour from this road will take you out for a closer look at the vast Jostedalsbreen icecap. Take a right turn from the centre of Loen onto the small, unmarked road to Kjenndal. The road will take you literally within a few hundred metres of the magnificent glacier, and provide fabulous views of the Loenvatn Lake as you ride. Returning to the E39 it is then a short ride to the small town of Stryn. Spend the night here in preparation for the fantastic riding ahead.

From Stryn, head a short distance east to the start of the Old Strynefjell Mountain Road, a 27 km (17 mile) narrow gravel road that twists through true wilderness. This is a journey through Norway's natural beauty at its most stunning; the road and the landscape almost one. Just as you think that it really cannot get any better, you hit the Golden Route, Norway's motorcycling nirvana. Firstly, a detour on a rough mountain toll road takes you to the Dalsnibba viewpoint, affording impressive views of the Geirangerfjord where spectacular waterfalls cascade down sheer cliffs into turquoise water and mountain farms cling to the rocks. Next is the Ornevegen ('Eagles' Highway'), a thrilling ride of multiple switchbacks. From Eidsdal, a short ferry ride connects to Linge and the start of the Trollstigen road. Mention this road to anyone who has ridden in Norway and they will break into a silly, glazed-eyed grin. This dizzying, white-knuckled rollercoaster of a ride zigzags through eleven hairpin bends across the face of the mountain and is an engineering masterpiece. Experience mountain climbing by motorcycle on one of the best roads you will ever ride. You will roll into the lovely coastal town of Andalsnes grinning from ear to ear.

BIKE: It is possible to take your own bike into Norway. You can hire bikes in Søgne, near Kristiansand. There are operators offering bike-inclusive tours.

WEATHER WATCH: Many passes are closed until June. June to August is the best time to visit, but the roads are quieter in June.

EXTENDING THE RIDE: Ferries from Stavanger connect to Newcastle on the northeast coast of England. From Newcastle head either south to Yorkshire or north to Scotland. Ferries from Bergen connect to Seydisfjördur in Iceland and Scotland's Shetland Isles.

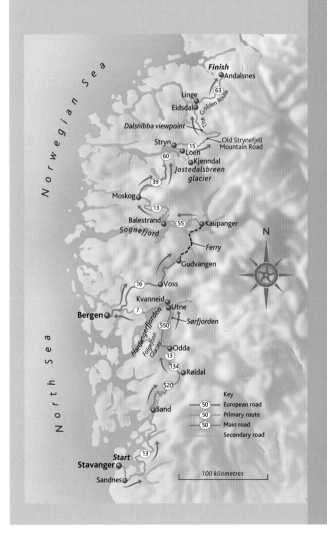

Edinburgh to Gairloch in the Northwest Highlands

Starting in Edinburgh, weave through Perthshire and the Great Glen to Gairloch on the northwest coast.

Once out of Edinburgh, Scotland's historic and beautiful capital, you soon find yourself riding in an unfolding landscape of soft hills and mist-shrouded glens, spectacular mountains and a wild, rugged coast. The subtle changing light is magical as morning mists lift to reveal mountains covered in purple heather and sharp granite peaks. The light changes throughout the day, creating an atmospheric backdrop to Scotland's untamed landscape.

Scotland feels wonderfully remote, yet distances across some of the best biking roads in Europe are often quite short. Single track roads twist across mountains, skirt around lochs and weave through glens, and it takes only minutes to slip away from the crowds onto deserted roads that lead across moors and to the craggy coastline and rocky beaches. For riders in search of solitude and days of long empty roads, Scotland is hard to beat.

▽ *Highland roads can be wonderfully empty.*

SCOTLAND EDINBURGH TO GAIRLOCH IN THE NORTHWEST HIGHLANDS

The Route

This route can easily be ridden in a few days, but allow a little longer if you wish to combine your riding with sightseeing and relaxing on the northwest coast.

An hour and a half's ride north of Edinburgh through Perthshire's soft glens and magnificent woodland brings you to Crieff, a genteel spa town and home of Glenturret, one of Scotland's oldest distilleries. From Crieff head west for a further 30 minutes to the village of Tyndrum, where you can refuel both yourself and the bike and use the helmet wash provided by the biker-friendly Green Welly Stop. It is a wild 50 km (31 mile) ride across Rannoch Moor, on a fabulous motorcycle road with long sweeping bends and a good, grippy surface. The A82 snakes across dramatic, desolate moorland to arrive at beautiful Glencoe, a magnificent, moody, mountain valley with a glorious and blood-thirsty history. Stay a few days and soak up the atmosphere whilst walking among the mountains.

Leave Glencoe, blasting north for about half an hour to Fort William. You are now deep into Highland territory and the Great Glen – a wall of mountains and lochs that cuts across

△ Glencoe has beautiful views and a blood-thirsty history.

147

▷ *Gairloch, in the far northwest of Scotland.*

the Highlands from Fort William north to Inverness. Slip off the main road at Invergarry just 40 km (25 miles) north of Fort William, and take an hour's ride west on a good, fast road that climbs high through forest, opening out to reveal magnificent views down to Loch Cluanie before snaking through the mountains of Glen Shiel, past the awesome Five Sisters of Kintail to one of Scotland's famous landmarks, Eilean Donan Castle. From here head north for 65 km (41 miles), winding your way around Loch Carron onto the Applecross Peninsula and the infamous Bealach na Ba – the 'Pass of the Cattle' – for an exhilarating ride of hair-raising switchbacks across bleak moorland. Challenging bends take you to the summit of the highest road in the highlands, ascending 625 m (2,050 ft) in just 10 km (6 miles); the views from the top are superb.

▽ BELOW LEFT *Catching the evening sun.*

▽ BELOW RIGHT *Eilean Donan Castle.*

Stay overnight in the village of Applecross, then ride north along the narrow single-track road that hugs the coast around the peninsula. The views are fabulous and an early start means you are likely to have this spectacular road all to yourself as you weave your way to Loch Torridon, the northern boundary of the peninsula. Just 12 km (8 miles) north of Torridon lie the beautiful pine-covered islands of Loch Maree. The dramatic and

imposing landscape that surrounds the loch unfolds as you skirt the shores on the A832, which then cuts inland and across to the coast. The village of Gairloch is situated around the shores of a beautiful sea loch looking west across to Skye and the Outer Hebrides. Ride out to long, sandy beaches set against a backdrop of the ancient Torridon Mountains, take a boat trip out to see abundant wildlife, or replace your bike boots with hiking boots and head up wonderful mountain paths. Gairloch has a wealth of accommodation and activities and makes a perfect base to explore the wild, beautiful coastline of Scotland's northwest.

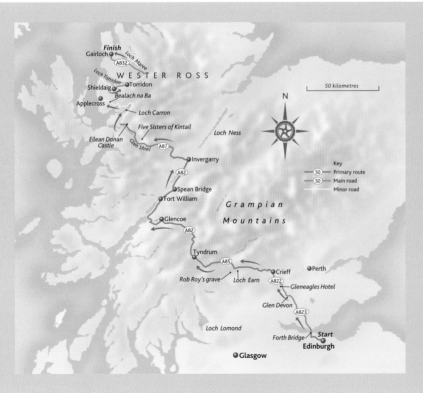

tool box

BIKE: It is possible to take your own bike into Scotland. Bike hire is available in Glasgow and Edinburgh. There are operators offering bike-inclusive tours.

WEATHER WATCH: April to September is the best time to visit.

EXTENDING THE RIDE: Cross the border into northern England. Take a boat from Stranraer near Glasgow to Belfast in Northern Ireland. Boats from Rosyth near Edinburgh to Belgium will get you into Europe. Boats depart from Scotland's remote Shetland Isles to Iceland and Norway.

Cork to the Cliffs of Moher

*From the lively city of Cork, ride southwest to the
three peninsulas, then north to the dramatic Cliffs of Moher.*

The southwest corner of the Emerald Isle is a magical land of soft, green hills and misty lakes. The spectacular craggy coast rises from the Atlantic, dropping to deserted beaches and encircling wild mountains. Welcoming pubs ring with infectious Irish humour and traditional live music.

Follow scenic roads that snake along the shoreline of the three peninsulas: wild and remote Beara; Iveragh with its famous Ring of Kerry; and finally the stunning Dingle Peninsula. Ride over scenic passes for breathtaking views, pull over at tranquil beaches or join in the 'craic' at lively towns and villages. This is an unhurried ride through a peaceful landscape, on paved roads that are often empty and sometimes a little bumpy, but seemingly contoured to the rolling hills they traverse.

▽ *One of Dingle's
lively bars.*

The Route

Daily distances are short, therefore a week will allow time for a leisurely ride and at least one night on each of the three peninsulas.

As you head west from Cork to the Beara Peninsula, the forested green countryside soon gives way to a wild, windswept landscape that at times feels almost alpine. If you want to stay on the peninsula try the popular village of Glengarriff, around 80 km (50 miles) from Cork. Traffic is light and you will have the roads to yourself as you head towards the tip of the peninsula. The highlight of any ride through the Beara is the Healy Pass, a narrow mountain road that cuts through the heart of the Caha Mountains affording breathtaking views from the summit.

From Kenmare at the head of the Beara peninsula, ride north to Killarney, a popular tourist town that plays host to Ireland Bike Week in late May. Join in the fun, sample the Guinness and pick up some tips from local riders before you ride the Ring of Kerry, the scenic 175 km (109 mile) road that encircles the Iveragh Peninsula. It is possibly

most famous road and therefore very popular. You may decide to ride the route clockwise to avoid constantly overtaking coach tours, but bear in mind that you may then meet the buses on the numerous blind corners. The road meanders past mountains and lakes and through picturesque villages. At Caherdaniel, on the southern point of the peninsula, the road climbs steeply up and over the Coomakista Pass affording superb views. Below the pass lies Derrynane Bay, a pleasant area to stay if you want to avoid the crowds.

As you ride across the northern rim of the peninsula there are great views across to Dingle Bay, your next destination. The Dingle Peninsula is sprinkled with archaeological sites and long sandy beaches. It is a predominantly Gaelic-speaking area, so road signs can get interesting. A direct and narrow 10 km (6 mile) road will take you from the Ring of Kerry across to Castlemaine on the peninsula's southern rim. Enjoy riding the long, straight

△ *The Ring of Kerry.*

BIKE: It is possible to take your own bike into Ireland. Due to prohibitive insurance costs, bike hire is very limited. It is easier to hire in Northern Ireland. There are operators offering tours.

WEATHER WATCH: May to September is the best time to visit.

EXTENDING THE RIDE: Catch a ferry from Dublin to England's northwest coast, or from Belfast to Stranraer near Glasgow.

ATLANTIC OCEAN

Cliffs of Moher ● **Finish**
R478
N67
Killimer
Tarbert
River Shannon
N69
N22 National Primary road
N69 National secondary road
R56 Regional road
Conor Pass
R560
N86
Tralee
R559
Dingle Peninsula
Dingle R561 Castlemaine
Annascaul
Slea Head
Dingle Bay
N70
Killarney
Iveragh Peninsula
N22
Ring of Kerry
R568 R569
N70 R571 Kenmare
Derrynane Bay
Caherdaniel R574 Glengarriff R584
Beara Peninsula
R572 Healy Pass

N

Key

Start
● **Cork**
R618

30 kilometres

road along the southern edge which passes the long, sandy beach at Inch and the famous South Pole Inn at the village of Annascaul. Dingle Town, with its beautiful harbour, places to stay and pubs that reverberate with traditional music, makes a great base.

Ride the stunning circuit around the tip of the peninsula along Slea Head, returning to Dingle Town to cross the steep narrow Conor Pass, which cuts across a ridge of mountains to the north coast, ascending over 500 m (1,640 ft) for fabulous views. Once over the Conor Pass ride east to Tralee at the head of the peninsula, then around 50 km (31 miles) north to Tarbert and catch the car ferry across the River Shannon to Killimer. Pick up the coastal road for around an hour to the mighty Cliffs of Moher, which rise 213 m (700 ft) out of the Atlantic Ocean. The dramatic wave-battered coastline is an awesome sight. Roll up for sunset and watch the sun's dying rays warm up the rocks before dipping below the Atlantic.

◁ *The Dingle Peninsula.*

▽ *The cliffs of Moher.*

Kendal to Whitby

From Kendal in the English Lake District, ride through the
Yorkshire Dales and the North York Moors to Whitby on the east coast.

North Yorkshire is one of the few places in England where you really can escape to a wild, wide-open land of heather-clad moors, limestone scars and pure, clean air. The untamed beauty and solitude of the moors will take your breath away, while ancient abbeys and formidable castles mark the landscape – yet drop down to the dales and you enter a soft countryside of historic market towns and pretty villages filled with blossom, where the local pubs serve real Yorkshire helpings and the tea shop rules supreme.

▽ *Riding across heather-clad moors.*

The roads in North Yorkshire are superb and offer some of the best biking in England, twisting and sweeping through sunny dales and across wild moors. The tarmac is generally good and views from the saddle are fabulous. Motorcycling is big in North Yorkshire, and biker-friendly cafés and pubs line the favourite routes. The roads really are a biking nirvana and can resemble a race track on a sunny Sunday, but take to the road mid-week or on a cool evening and you will have them all to yourself.

△ ABOVE LEFT *One of Yorkshire's many tea shops.*

△ ABOVE RIGHT *Picturesque villages dot this route.*

The Route

This journey features just a taste of the superb riding and stunning scenery you can expect from a ride in North Yorkshire. The following route can be ridden in a day, but two days will allow time for sightseeing.

From Kendal in the Lake District the A684 runs east over the Pennines and into the Yorkshire Dales. It is a very popular motorcycling road, combining hairpins, sweeping bends and reasonably fast straights on good, smooth tarmac. The first 44 km (27 miles) to the village of Hawes is great fun and Hawes is also a popular hiking and biking centre, so pull over for a drink and watch the bikes roll through the village. From Hawes, continue for a further 26 km (16 miles) on the A684 to Leyburn. Alternatively take the high single-track road that loops through the rugged heart of Swaledale, providing far-reaching views as you ride for around

tool box

BIKE: It is possible to take your own bike into England. Bike hire is available in Bolton, near Manchester or Shipley near Leeds. There are operators offering tours.

WEATHER WATCH: April to October is the best time to visit.

EXTENDING THE RIDE: Ride north to Newcastle and take a ferry to Norway, continue riding north into Scotland, or take a ferry from Liverpool to Dublin.

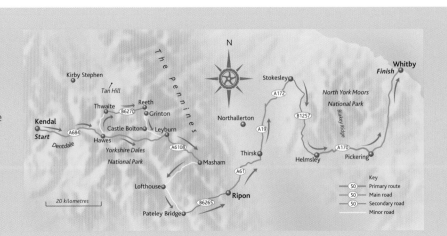

Kirby Stephen
Tan Hill
The Pennines
N
Stokesley
Whitby
Finish
A172
North York Moors
National Park
Thwaite
Reeth
B6270
Grinton
A19
B1257
Blakey Ridge
Kendal
Start
Castle Bolton
Leyburn
Northallerton
A684
Dentdale
Hawes
A6108
A170
Pickering
Yorkshire Dales
National Park
Masham
Thirsk
Helmsley
A61
Lofthouse
Ripon
Pateley Bridge
B6265
20 kilometres

Key
50 Primary route
50 Main road
50 Secondary road
Minor road

△ Perfect English motorcycling.

50 km (31 miles) north over the Buttertubs to the village of Thwaite, then east to Reeth and high over wild Redmire Moor. The imposing walls of Bolton Castle loom into view as you drop down off the moor to rejoin the A684 as it leads into the market town of Leyburn.

Head to Masham on the A6108, a short ride of around 18 km (11 miles). The landscape is softer as the road winds through the lovely town of Middleham, famous for its medieval castle and racing stables, and then on to Masham, the home of the Theakstons and Black Sheep breweries. From Masham the scenery is simply stunning as the road winds for 30 km (20 miles) over the moors, past crystal-clear reservoirs and the pretty village of Lofthouse before descending to Pateley Bridge, a popular pull-in for motorcyclists riding in from the excellent roads that surround the town. From Pateley Bridge, 19 km (12 miles) of fast straights and sweeping bends take you to the tiny cathedral city of Ripon. There is plenty of accommodation in and around the city.

Start the following day with a big Yorkshire breakfast, then head towards the North York Moors and the North Sea coast. From Ripon, a 20-minute ride east takes you to the market town of Thirsk, famous as the home of James Herriot, the author of *All Creatures Great and Small*. From Thirsk take a short ride northeast to Stokesley for the start of a superb 32 km (20 mile) run of smooth tarmac and sweeping bends through valleys and woodland to Helmsley, another popular pull-in. From Helmsley it is a great hour's ride over the heather-clad North York Moors to the east coast town of Whitby, famous for its connections with Captain Cook and Bram Stoker's *Dracula*. The cliff-top abbey dominates the town, and views from the coastal path are superb. Whitby's other claim to fame is the Magpie fish and chip shop, so park up, join the queue and then wander along the pier with your deliciously fresh fish and chips.

◁ Whitby, with its famous abbey visible at the top of the hill.

157

The Nürburgring

Enjoy the scenery of the German Wine Route, then head northwest to the Nürburgring.

Experience the thrill of riding the longest and possibly the most demanding circuit in the world. The Ring is legendary and a piece of racing history. Opened in 1927, the circuit was designed as the ultimate challenge to test the world's best riders and drivers. The Nürburgring or Nordschleife is also one of the most beautiful circuits, winding its way through lovely Rhineland countryside. Imagine the combined joy of riding on a long mountain road that is also a race track, perfect ingredients to get the heart pumping. If you've always wanted to experience the adrenaline rush of riding a race circuit, then this is the opportunity of a lifetime.

▽ *The scenic roads of the Moselle Valley.*

△ ABOVE LEFT *Boppard am Rhein*.

△ ABOVE RIGHT *Cochem Imperial Castle, in the Moselle Valley*.

The Nürburgring lies 90 km (56 miles) southwest of Cologne in the mountainous Eifel region of the Rhineland, a superb region for motorcycling. Sweeping, well-surfaced roads cut through a landscape of rolling hills, valleys lined with vineyards, crater lakes and extensive wooded slopes. There are bike-friendly hotels along the way and close to the Ring, providing lockable parking, drying rooms and often repair services. If you are travelling alone, it is a great way to meet fellow motorcyclists, as you can be sure that some of your fellow travellers will be heading to the Ring.

The Route

Combine a ride around the Ring with a few days touring the Rhineland.

Start in Schweigen on the French border, riding north following the Deutsche Weinstrasse – the 'German Wine Route' – to Bockenheim for around 125 km (78 miles). Medieval castles and fortresses dominate a region of cobblestone villages and beautifully preserved historic towns surrounded by vine-clad slopes and forested hills. Leaving the Wine Route at Bockenheim it is a 114 km (71 mile) ride north to the pretty town of Boppard, on the banks of the Rhine. Spend the night here, rising early for the short 46 km (29 miles) ride to the Nürburgring – just far enough to warm up the tyres.

The Ring was originally built as a combined test track and race circuit. When not in use it was made available for public use, a practice that continues to this day. It is officially a one-way public toll road, and German road rules apply on the track. You can ride any type of motorcycle, but it must be road legal. There is no speed limit but there is a noise limit of 95 decibels. Tickets are available on site, starting at 20 euros a lap, although the seriously obsessed can obtain an annual ticket. You turn up, pay your money and ride the lap of a lifetime. There are 21 km (13 miles) of track with 73 bends – that's 33 left- and 40 right-handers, so don't forget your knee-sliders. The Ring is no modern race circuit, but a series of blind bends, steep inclinations and constantly changing road surfaces. This is an unforgiving

▽ BELOW LEFT *The Nürburgring.*

▽ BELOW RIGHT *Riding the German Wine Route.*

and demanding circuit, so be realistic about your riding capabilities. There are training schemes aimed at teaching you the perfect techniques for taking to the track with confidence and making the most of this amazing circuit. It isn't a race, and there's no champagne at the end unless you bring your own. It is just the incredible opportunity to ride in the tracks of some of the world's best riders and drivers. Relax and enjoy the experience of riding one of motor racing's legendary circuits.

BIKE: It is possible to take your own bike into Germany. Bike hire is available in Cologne and other major cities. There are operators offering bike-inclusive tours, and hotels that offer guided routes.

WEATHER WATCH: See http://www.nuerburgring.de for opening dates.

EXTENDING THE RIDE: Head across to Zurich for a ride around the Alps or head into France.

Annecy Circuit via the Côte d'Azur

From Annecy in the Rhone-Alpes, ride the historic Route Napoléon through Provence to the Côte d'Azur, returning to Annecy over the high alpine passes that skirt the Italian border.

The diversity of the landscape in the southeast corner of France will surprise anyone visiting for the first time. It boasts mighty alpine peaks and high-altitude passes that stretch as far as the chic resorts of the Côte d'Azur on the Mediterranean coast, whilst rural Provence is covered with lavender fields and lovely hilltop towns and villages. Wherever you ride and whatever your budget, the fabulous food and wine will be an additional highlight of any visit to the region.

▽ *Riding in the French Alps.*

France is a firm favourite with European motorcyclists due to race-track smooth roads that fly through a constantly changing landscape. The toll roads are fast and generally in excellent condition, while high passes twist over the Alps in a series of tight hairpins, swooping down to beautiful valleys. The temptation to be throttle-happy is high, but be warned – speeding fines are on the spot and the *gendarmes* will happily fine you if caught.

△ *Annecy, a beautiful town in the south of France.*

The Route

The following route can be ridden in two days, with an overnight stop on the Côte d'Azur. Alternatively allow a few extra days and flavour the fantastic riding with sightseeing in the mountains and rural Provence.

The beautiful town of Annecy lies on the shores of the Lac d'Annecy. Surrounded by mountains, its stunning location, set within the French Alps and close to the Swiss and Italian Alps, makes it a popular destination. It is also a great starting point for the 105 km (65 mile) ride south to Grenoble and the beginning of the historic Route Napoléon, which follows the route taken by Napoléon Bonaparte in 1815, following his exile on Elba. Generally considered one of the best bike roads in Europe, the N85 starts in the mountains

△ ABOVE LEFT *The glamorous Côte d'Azur.*

△ ABOVE RIGHT *Cime de la Bonette.*

and passes through dramatic scenery as it sweeps south to the Mediterranean via Digne-les-Bains and Castellane, gateway to the magnificent Gorges du Verdon. This is an excellent fast road, perfect for sports bikes. The tarmac is superb, and the corners a sublime combination of seriously fast sweepers and mountain hairpins. You are guaranteed to grin all the way. At just over 300 km (190 miles) from the Côte d'Azur, you will have time to lunch at one of Provence's pretty hilltop villages before spending the early evening cruising the Riviera, or chasing sports cars along the three corniche roads that run through the heart of the French Riviera.

Spend the night in Nice and leave early the next day, riding north for around an hour into the rugged peaks and valleys of the Mercantour National Park, a little-known region that offers peace and tranquillity after the hedonistic pleasures of the Côte d'Azur. At its heart the cobbled streets of St-Martin-Vésubie provide accommodation,

BIKE: It is possible to take your own bike into France. Bike hire is available throughout France. There are operators offering bike-inclusive tours.

WEATHER WATCH: May to September is the best time to visit. Some of the higher passes are closed until well into June. Traffic is at its heaviest from late July to late August.

EXTENDING THE RIDE: It is a short ride to the Swiss and Italian Alps. Alternatively head southwest to the Pyrenees.

food and wine. It is a 110 km (68 mile) ride through the Tinée Valley to Barcelonnette over the Cime de la Bonette (2,800 m/9,186 ft), a road that climbs almost into the clouds as it snakes past silent peaks, the clouds occasionally parting to offer magical views. Enjoy lunch at Barcelonnette's pretty café-lined square, then head north for about 300 km (186 miles) via the tight hairpins and steep ascents and descents of the Col d'Izoard and the Col du Galibier, finally returning to Annecy in the early evening. Take a short ride out of town to one of the picturesque lakeside villages and enjoy a well-earned candlelit supper by the side of the lake.

Bilbao to Perpignan Loop

From the Spanish Atlantic coastline to the French Mediterranean and back, this route takes in the best of the mountain roads on both sides of the Pyrenees, the tiny Principality of Andorra and a healthy slice of Catalonia.

Forming a stunning natural border between France and Spain, the Pyrenees are a motorcyclist's dream. Switchbacks and hairpins sweep over the mountains that divide the two countries and, at just over 400 km (248 miles) long and 50 km (31 miles) broad at the widest point, it is possible to breakfast on coffee and croissants in France, have tapas for lunch in Spain and return to France to dine on the *plat du jour* washed down with locally produced wine. The Principality of Andorra, wedged between the two, is completely encircled by mountains. Added to the fantastic riding is the change in landscape, climate and culture as you ride from the Atlantic to the Mediterranean, or cross the border using the numerous mountain passes.

▽ *Riding with friends in the Pyrenees.*

Motorcyclists are spoilt for choice: the roads are fantastic whatever direction you arrive from or head to. Go to Barcelona in June for the Moto GP, replace those leathers with some tax-free shopping in Andorra, and top it all riding some of the most superb motorcycling roads in Europe. Road surfaces are generally excellent and often traffic-free, especially in Spain. Snow-topped peaks, limestone pinnacles and medieval castles tower over roads that lead to glaciers, lakes and secluded valleys. There are sweeping bends, hairpins and long fast straights, corkscrew loops, uphill climbs and tricky, twisty turns, ensuring your knee-sliders work overtime!

The Route

This route will give you a flavour of both the French and Spanish sides of the Pyrenees and should take roughly two weeks, allowing time to combine your riding with some sightseeing.

△ *Playa del Sardinero, San Sebastian.*

Rolling off the boat at Bilbao you are straight into green Spain. If you prefer to take it easy on your first day while you find your land legs, a quick 100 km (63 mile) blast gets you to San Sebastián a little further along the coast. This is a town famous throughout Spain for its cuisine. Spend a lazy afternoon on the beach then treat yourself to a celebratory meal of *pintxos* (Basque tapas) at one of the great restaurants in the old town.

The next day, pack a picnic and get an early start on the N240 heading towards the town of Jaca. It is a good road with great views and it can easily be ridden in a day whether you start from Bilbao or San Sebastián. The lakeside section between Yesa and Puente la Reina de Jaca is particularly lovely, so unpack that picnic you brought with you and enjoy the scenery. There are some stunning roads in the area that snake through valleys to beautiful secluded villages. The Valle de Hecho and Valle de Ansó lie just northwest of Jaca and there is now a road connecting the two. Jaca is a fairly large and lively town and it makes a good base from which to explore the western Pyrenees.

At Jaca you join the legendary N260. This is the ultimate biking road. Well-surfaced, it wriggles all the way to the Mediterranean coast and up to the French border. A five hour ride on this fabulous road brings you to La Seu d'Urgell. From here head north into Andorra, stop for coffee, do some shopping and stay the night before dropping back into Spain at

Bourg-Madame. From here get on to the Coilada de Toses. This is a joy to ride – 40 km (28 miles) of fast bends on perfect tarmac and a favourite with locals. Meet other riders at the mid-way car park, swap route notes and race into Ripoll for lunch. If you've timed your ride to coincide with the annual Moto GP in June, cut south from Ripoll to the race track just outside Barcelona. It is a reasonably fast 104 km (65 miles) and should take just a couple of hours. Join thousands of fans at one of the world's most atmospheric and fun race days. The enthusiasm of the Spanish fans has to be experienced – they are truly crazy about their motorcycle racing and stage a fantastic event. Barcelona itself is a classic European city packed with sights and culture.

From Barcelona head north back into the Pyrenees, or continue from Ripoll along the N260. Either way you will ride through Figueres, Salvador Dalí's home town and the location of the Teatre-Museu Dalí, a must if you have any interest in surrealist art. From here follow the N260 as it twists along the coast, merging into the

BIKE: It is possible to take your own bike into France and Spain. Bike hire is available in major French and Spanish cities, including Bilbao. There are operators offering bike-inclusive tours.

WEATHER WATCH: Daytime temperatures are pleasant March to May and mid-to late September. June to August is hot and the crowds increase.

EXTENDING THE RIDE: Continue your riding in southeast France, or from Bilbao head south to Andalucía.

N114 as you cross the border into France and the town of Perpignan. The riding either side of the eastern Pyrenees is a motorcycling playground, so unpack for a few days and play on the passes. Biker-run hotels in charming villages perched high in the hills make a great base for you to sample locally produced food and wine, and meet other riders.

From Perpignan start out on the D117 and you cannot go wrong. A 75 km (48 mile) ride west takes you to Quillan, where the road starts to climb quickly towards Foix, and is then followed by a quick ride through sweeping bends to Saint-Girons. The riding is superb as the D618 threads through a succession of narrow mountain passes towards the Col d'Aspin. The fantastic riding continues as the D918 weaves for about 250 km (155 miles) through the French Pyrenees towards the Atlantic. At any point along this road you can take a twisty, hairpin pass that will climb up and then drop over the mountains into Spain for your return to the port at Bilbao. This is a region that, once discovered, you will return to time and again, finding new riding routes each visit.

◁ FAR LEFT *Winding through the Pyrenees.*

△ ABOVE *Park up and admire the views.*

A Circuit of Andalucía

Starting in Malaga, this route takes in the Sierra Nevada mountains, the Parque Natural de Cazorla, the Moorish cities of Cordoba and Seville and the wild Costa de la Luz, returning to Malaga via the Sierra de Grazalema.

▽ *The magnificent Alhambra palace in Grenada.*

This is the land of fiestas and fun-loving people. The riding is relaxed and the sun always seems to shine. Spend your days circling the switchbacks of the sierras and exploring the unique Moorish architecture, and your evenings enjoying the party atmosphere of Andalucía's towns and villages.

The Spanish are passionate about bikes, ensuring a warm welcome to visiting motorcyclists. Roads are well paved with plenty of curves and twists in the mountain ranges. The whole region is criss-crossed by off-road trails, so if you've never ridden off-road but would like to try it, then Spain is a great place to learn. Add to this the long sandy beaches, historic cities, great food and wine, and you have a winning blend. For a holiday combined with great riding, Andalucía is hard to beat.

△ ABOVE LEFT *Good weather is almost guaranteed in Spain.*

△ ABOVE RIGHT *Despite winding hairpin roads, the riding is relaxed here.*

The Route

The following route gives you a taste of Moorish Spain and can be ridden in a week, but allow longer if you wish to combine riding with sightseeing, relaxing on the beach or exploring the national parks.

From Malaga it is around a 100 km (62 mile) ride to the twisty mountain roads of the Sierra Nevada and the valleys of Las Alpujarras. Ride over beautiful mountain passes and enjoy panoramic views, and when you have finished playing on the superb roads drop down from the mountains to the Moorish city of Granada, its star attraction the magnificent Alhambra palace, framed against a backdrop of the Sierra Nevada mountains. Granada is a beautiful city, so stay a few days before heading northeast for around 200 km (125 miles) to the Parque Natural de Cazorla for spectacular scenic riding on paved and dirt roads.

▷ *The city of Ronda, in the Spanish province of Malaga.*

From Cazorla the road winds over the 1200 m (4,000 ft) Puerto de las Palomas ('Mountain Pass of the Doves') and down to Empalme del Valle, where it turns north to follow the Guadalquivir Valley. Pick up the N322 for around two hours to Cordoba, where you can lose yourself in the labyrinthine old quarter surrounding the 8th century Mezquita. Unless you yearn for a blast along the highway, take the scenic sweeping A431 for 130 km (81 miles) to Seville, Andalucía's capital city. Dine at a table on the cobbled streets, take a horse-drawn carriage between sights and cruise the Rio Guadalquivir as the sun sets.

From Seville, head an hour south to the lovely town of Jerez de la Frontera. In May the race circuit here attracts thousands of spectators from all over Europe for the Jerez Moto GP. If you need proof that the Spanish love motorcycling, just join the crowds and get caught up in all the excitement.

From Jerez ride southeast along the Costa de la Luz – the wild, unspoilt face of Andalucía with its white, sandy beaches and jagged cliffs. Surging ocean waves provide a constant cool breeze – a welcome relief if you have been riding in Andalucía's hot, dry centre.

Spend the night in the town of Tarifa on Andalucía's southern tip then take a ride north to Ronda, which sits astride the El Tajo Gorge and amongst the Serrania de Ronda mountains. The scenic route takes you through the Parque Natural Los Alcornocales and into the Sierra de Grazalema Natural Park on a road that twists and turns as it climbs, then drops to long, sweeping bends.

△ *The Jerez Moto GP attracts large crowds.*

The views are spectacular and the landscape constantly changing as the cork forests are replaced by rugged limestone cliffs, gullies and gorges. In spring, mimosa and almond blossom sweeten the air as the road sweeps towards Ronda, a popular pull-in for motorcyclists. Stop for lunch and spectacular views of the gorge before joining yet another scenic, sweeping road east, taking you 100 km (62 miles) back to Malaga and the Mediterranean coast.

BIKE: It is possible to take your own bike into Spain. Malaga and Seville offer a wide choice of bike hire. There are operators offering bike-inclusive tours both on- and off-road.

WEATHER WATCH: March to May and mid- to late September offer pleasant daytime temperatures. Avoid June to August when it is crowded and very hot.

EXTENDING THE RIDE: Take the ferry to Morocco from Tarifa or Algeciras. Alternatively head north into the Pyrenees.

The Swiss Alps to the Austrian Tyrol

Start in Switzerland, dip briefly into Italy, then ride up into the Austrian Tyrol.

The Alps stretch from Austria and Slovenia in the east, through Switzerland, Liechtenstein, Italy and Germany to France in the west. The region boasts a pristine beauty, crisp mountain air and some of the most gorgeous mountains in the world, including the formidable Matterhorn and the beautiful Mont Blanc.

The Alps have to be the most famous motorcycling region in Europe. Perfectly engineered roads cut through the heart of the mountains, offering challenging, exciting riding alongside breathtaking mountain scenery. Switzerland alone has 72 passes on an unending spiral of perfect tarmac. Italy's Passo dello Stelvio is hairpin heaven, and Austria is home to the famous Grossglockner Pass, a not-to-be-missed motorcycle experience.

The Route

The following route can easily be ridden in four days and is just a taste of the thrilling riding you can expect in the Alps.

Start with a fairly short day of around 200 km (125 miles). It should take you about an hour and a half to ride from Zurich to the mountain resort of Meiringen. Pull over and enjoy excellent alpine views over lunch before the afternoon fun begins. First is the dramatic Grimsel Pass, followed closely by the 2,431 m (7,975 ft) climb over the Furka Pass with its fabulous views of the Rhône Glacier. This is a ride of multiple switchbacks and knuckle-whitening hairpins that carve through the mountains on a thrilling serpentine road, guaranteed to get the adrenaline going and your gearbox working overtime. Descend the pass and ride into the town of Andermatt. Surrounded by mountains it is a popular stop-over with motorcyclists, so park up for the night, talk bikes and share a beer with other riders.

Clock up around 300 km (186 miles) as you leave Andermatt and head south over the famous St Gotthard Pass and weave through the mountains on some of the finest roads

▽ *The Furka Pass has amazing views.*

△ *Andermatt is a popular stopping place for motorcyclists.*

you can ride. Pass through the lovely old town of Bellinzona, climb up over the 2,063 m (6,768 ft) San Bernardino Pass, then east and onto the hairpins of the Splügen Pass, taking you over the Swiss/Italian border to the lovely town of Chiavenna. Wine, meats and cheeses matured in the rocks surrounding the town are a local speciality, so park up at one of the outdoor cafés and enjoy panoramic views and regional fare while your engine cools ready for the afternoon's ride. Cross back into Switzerland and ride past the forests, lakes and snow-capped peaks of the breathtakingly beautiful Engadine Valley. Splash out and spend a night at the glitzy resort of St Moritz, or continue 35 km (21 miles) north to the peaceful little town of Zernez, close to the alpine wilderness of the Parc Naziunal Svizzer.

From Zernaz, HW28 takes you southeast for around 100 km (62 miles) over the Italian border towards the spa town of Merano, passing the entrance to Passo dello Stelvio, at 2,757 m (9,045 ft) the highest paved mountain pass in the eastern Alps. It boasts an incredible 42 hairpins on the ascent, so if the temptation is too much, take a day's detour

BIKE: It is possible to take your own bike into Switzerland. Bike hire is available in Zurich. There are operators offering bike-inclusive tours.

WEATHER WATCH: Most passes open in June until October. Traffic is at its heaviest from late July to late August.

EXTENDING THE RIDE: From Lienz take a short ride southwest to Cortina d'Ampezzo in the Italian Dolomites, or cross into Slovenia over the Wurzen Pass.

to ride this amazing pass. Continuing from Merano climb northwest over the steep, narrow Timmelsjoch Pass into Austria. Spend the night in lively Innsbruck, capital of the Austrian Tyrol, ready for the ride of your life the next day on the 3,798 m (12,460 ft) Grossglockner Pass.

From Innsbruck it is around a three hour ride to Fusch and the start of the Grossglockner. This pass extends a very warm welcome to riders, with information, parking and free lockers provided along the way. You can almost reach out and touch the peaks as you negotiate an amazing 39 hairpins over 48 km (30 miles). Perfect your cornering on the sweeping, smooth asphalt and grin from ear to ear as you hone your riding skills on a continuing parade of fabulous mountainous hairpins. Leave the Grossglockner and head to the café-filled square of Lienz, a picturesque town close to the Italian border, over which the rose-tinted pinnacles of the Dolomites await.

◁ FAR LEFT *Stunning Alpine scenery.*

◁ LEFT *Riding through the Alps.*

▽ *The dramatic Grimsel Pass.*

The Dolomites

Ride the fabled Great Dolomites Road from Bolzano through the heart of the Dolomites to Cortina d'Ampezzo.

Located in northern Italy, the Dolomites are dramatic, jagged rocky pinnacles that rise high above forested valleys filled with wild flowers and emerald lakes. The spectacular roads that link the mountain ranges wind through breathtaking scenery and pretty flower-filled villages.

▽ *Carezza Lake.*

△ ABOVE LEFT *Cortina d'Ampezzo.*

△ ABOVE RIGHT *The sweeping roads of the Dolomites.*

There are very few straight roads in the Dolomites. Sheer, vertical rock faces tower above the excellent tarmac that hugs the base of the mountains. The surrounding views are stunning, making it difficult to keep your eyes on the road, but it is definitely the warm Italian welcome that makes motorcycling in this region so special. Almost every hotel or restaurant will have signs proclaiming 'Bikers Welcome' and offering special 'Biker Menus'. Hotels display an orange sign with a motorcycle logo proclaiming *moto sotto il tetto* ('bike under the roof'), and offer secure parking, touring information and often spa facilities designed to ease your limbs after a long day's ride. Make the most of the fantastic hospitality and get yourself a base for a few days. Unpack your kit, meet other riders staying at the hotel and watch the towering peaks turn rose pink at sunset as you plan the next day's ride from the comfort of the hotel bar.

The Route

This is a classic riding route, combined with side trips on roads that wind over fabulous passes and past vertical rock faces. This is a day's ride covering around 150 km (93 miles) and provides just a taste of the riding in store.

Start in the beautiful old town of Bolzano, heading southeast on the Great Dolomites Road towards Carezza Lake, where the jagged spires of the Latemar and Catinaccio chains reflect in its tranquil waters. From Carezza the road climbs towards the Passo Costalunga, but a few kilometres before the top, take the turn towards Passo Nigra, gently descending

BIKE: It is possible to take your own bike into Italy. Bike hire is available in Venice and Verona, and other major cities. There are operators offering bike-inclusive tours and hotels that offer guided routes.

WEATHER WATCH: June to September is the best time to visit. August is crowded and best avoided.

EXTENDING THE RIDE: From Cortina d'Ampezzo cross the border into Austria or Slovenia.

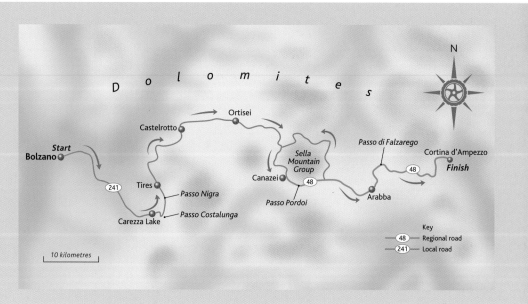

D o l o m i t e s

N

Ortisei

Castelrotto

Start
Bolzano

Sella
Mountain
Group

Passo di Falzarego

Cortina d'Ampezzo

48

Finish

241

Tires

Canazei

48

Passo Nigra

Passo Costalunga

Passo Pordoi

Arabba

Carezza Lake

Key

48 — Regional road

241 — Local road

10 kilometres

to the town of Tires some 8 km (5 miles) away. Stop for a cappuccino and admire the breathtaking views.

Back on the bike, the views are stupendous as you take a right turn heading towards Ortisei on a steadily winding uphill road via Castelrotto. Look out for the road to the Rifugio Bellavista, which lies at 1,884 m (6,181 ft) on a 10 km (6 mile) road of spiralling bends that promises some knee-down action. Refuges are renowned for their simple, tasty food, not to mention the fantastic views. Stop here for lunch before continuing on to Ortisei.

From Ortisei the SS242 heads towards the Sella mountain group. The fabulous loop of the passes that surround these stunning peaks is a joy to ride – the road must have been designed by a motorcyclist. Once you've ridden the loop – possibly a few times! – rejoin the Great Dolomites Road at the town of Canazei as it continues east over high passes. First up is the Passo Pordoi, boasting over 30 hairpins on the eastern ramp. The pass leads to the town of Arabba, a popular pull-in for bikers. Ease off the throttle as you ride through a number of small towns before the road climbs up over the Passo di Falzarego – a combination of sweepers, hairpins and fast straights descending to the lively town of Cortina d'Ampezzo, which is surrounded by some of the most magnificent mountains of the Dolomites. Relax with a cool drink in the town square as you watch the stream of motorcycles thundering down from the passes. Quite simply *moto-bellissimo*!

◁ *The Sella mountain group, part of the Dolomites.*

▽ *Although beautiful in winter, the Dolomites are best visited in warmer months on a bike.*

Ljubljana to Lake Bled

*Ride to the vineyards of eastern Slovenia, the karst landscape
of the Soca Valley and the mountains of Triglav National Park.*

Nestled between the Alps and the Adriatic Sea, Slovenia is one of Europe's smallest and loveliest countries. At the heart of Europe, this little-known country of wild ancient forests and glacial lakes is the perfect antidote to the summer crowds. The limestone peaks and green valleys in the northwest are the most southerly extension of the great alpine range which sweeps across from neighbouring Austria and Italy. To the east, soft hillsides swathed with vineyards roll towards the warm waters of the Adriatic.

At barely 300 km (186 miles) wide, Slovenia may be small but it has big landscapes. Rural towns and villages provide inexpensive accommodation and a friendly welcome, and

▽ *Riding in the
Logarska Valley.*

there is a relaxed feel to a journey in this beautiful, peaceful country. Road surfaces are generally very good, although some of the small back roads can be a little rough. Traffic is much lighter this side of the Alps and you will find yourself riding on empty roads that lead over vine-covered hills into forested valleys and high over alpine passes.

The Route

The following route should take about a week, but allow a little longer if you want to explore the national parks.

Ljubljana, Slovenia's capital city, is small but lively, making it an enjoyable place to spend a few days. Restaurants and bars spill out onto the narrow streets, and cafés line the river. Leaving the city, the medieval town of Skofja Loka is just a half hour's ride northwest and certainly worth a visit. From here, head northeast for around 100 km (62 miles) to the beautiful glacial Logarska Valley in the Kamniske-Savinja Alps, a lovely area to stop for lunch and perhaps take a short walk. Continue heading east for around two hours, mainly on motorway, to Ljutomer and the start of Slovenia's Wine Road. The short but scenic road

▽ *A hillside vineyard at Jeruzalem.*

winds for just under 20 km (12 miles) through picturesque terraced vineyards, via the lovely hilltop village of Jeruzalem and on to Ormoz. Jeruzalem was named by crusaders in the 13th century, enamoured by the beauty of the area and its fine wines. Stay in the village overnight and sample the wines in this lovely, tranquil location.

From Ormoz, head south via the historic city of Ptuj for around 270 km (169 miles) on the small, scenic roads that wind through pristine forest and the wine-growing regions of eastern Slovenia. It will take you most of the day to reach Postojna, the closest town for visiting the huge chambers of the Postojna Caves and the medieval Predjama Castle, dramatically perched halfway up a 130 m (426 ft) cliff. From here it is a short ride to the Skocjan Caves, a UNESCO World Heritage Site and one of Slovenia's most stunning natural attractions.

From Postojna head northwest for around 100 km (62 miles) to the lovely Soca Valley, where the emerald green river flows from limestone peaks. The town of Bovec is a centre for adventure sports within the valley and provides a good range of accommodation options. From Bovec ride the spectacular Vrsic Pass, the highest mountain pass in Slovenia. The scenic 25 km (16 mile) route cuts through alpine scenery in a series of 50 fantastic hairpin bends linking Bovec and Kranjska Gora in the Triglav National Park, from where it is just a 45 minute ride to the lakeside town of Bled, on the fringe of the Julian Alps. The lake is surrounded by snow-covered mountains and, with a fairytale castle perched on the northern shore and a tiny island at its centre, it is a stunning place to relax while you decide whether to head to the Italian Dolomites or the Austrian Alps.

▷ RIGHT *Triglav National Park.*

▽ BELOW LEFT *Pausing for lunch in a town square in Slovenia.*

▽ BELOW RIGHT *Lake Bled, the end of your journey.*

BIKE: It is possible to take your own bike into Slovenia. Bike hire is available in Ljubljana. There are operators offering bike-inclusive tours.

WEATHER WATCH: May to September is the best time to visit.

EXTENDING THE RIDE: Cross into Italy and continue your ride in the Italian Dolomites, or head into Austria for a ride around the Alps.

Istanbul Loop via Anatolia and the Coast

From Istanbul head east to the lunar landscapes of central Anatolia, through the Taurus Mountains and along the Turquoise Coast. Then head north along the Aegean Coast, returning to Istanbul via the Dardanelles.

△ *Posing for the camera in Turkey.*

This is a country steeped in layers of history and legends. Ruins of the Roman and Byzantine Empires lie scattered along the Mediterranean and Aegean coasts, and Cappadocia's troglodyte Christian churches and lunar landscape enthral visitors to central Anatolia. You can also watch the Whirling Dervishes of Konya and discover the ancient city of Troy.

The warmth and friendliness of the Turkish people make a motorcycle journey through Turkey a rewarding and pleasurable experience. Stopping to ask the way often results in a place at the *tavla* (backgammon) table, drinks on the house or an invitation to meet friends and family. The hospitality is genuine and gracious, and will accompany you from the metropolis of Istanbul through coastal towns and sleepy villages. Turkish hospitality is matched by its delicious and varied cuisine. Even on the quietest of back roads you are never far from a restaurant or café, often the hub of the village and an ideal place to meet people.

For the Turkish people, motorcycling as a hobby is a relatively new phenomenon and you are now more likely to meet Turkish riders discovering their country by motorcycle than ever before. Road conditions vary from smooth, fast motorways linking the main cities, to bumpy rural roads. Major roads are not regularly maintained and can quickly switch from perfect to potholed tarmac, but the pace is never fast and the distances between towns not huge. Once discovered, lunch at a *lokanta* (restaurant) will become a highlight of your day's ride, and you will quickly get into a relaxed riding pace.

The Route

Turkey is a huge and vastly varied country offering endless motorcycling possibilities. If you've got two weeks, try the following leisurely 3,000 km (1,864 mile) loop from Istanbul.

Istanbul has to be one of the most beautiful cities in the world, so linger a few days to appreciate her many charms. Riding through Istanbul's densely packed ancient streets is hair-raising, but someone will always point you in the right direction and, once out on the open road, the pace is leisurely and traffic is generally light. It will take about an hour to ride out of the city to the ferry terminal at Eskihisar for a 30 minute crossing of the Sea of Marmara to Topcular or, if you wish to avoid riding in the city traffic, you can cross from Yenikapi in the old city to Yalova or Bandirma. Rolling off the ferry you are straight onto lovely mountain roads that wind for 180 km (112 miles) via the eastern tip of Lake Iznik to Bursa, nestling in the lower slopes of Uluda Mountain. Famous as first capital of the Ottoman Empire, Bursa also has a well deserved reputation for its delicious Iskender kebab and *kestane sekeri*, chestnut-based sweets. Spend the evening wandering the bazaars buying local delicacies to store in your tank bag.

Heading northeast, the road to Safranbolu follows valleys, lakes and mountains (via Bozüyük and Bolu) for almost 450 km (280 miles). Picnic on the treats you bought at the bazaars as you stop to enjoy the views. Safranbolu is a beautifully preserved Ottoman town, and also a UNESCO World Heritage Site. Soak in 17th century baths and spend the night in a restored Ottoman house. It is a full day's ride to the unique landscape of the central Anatolian plateau. The road winds through the beautiful mountain passes of the Western Black Sea Mountains, dropping on to the volcanic landscapes of Cappadocia. Ride through valleys of strangely eroded rock formations to cave churches adorned with frescos, and underground cities carved in the soft volcanic rock. Accommodation options in Göreme and Urgüp are plentiful and varied. Stay in a cave hotel – lovely and cool during the day, their vantage points often command the most fantastic views of the ever-changing colours of the

▽ *Cappadocia's volcanic landscape.*

BIKE: It is possible to take your own bike into Turkey. Bike hire is available in Istanbul and Ankara. There are operators offering bike-inclusive tours.

WEATHER WATCH: Daytime temperatures are pleasant in early May and mid-September. June to August is very hot and the crowds increase along the coast at this time.

EXTENDING THE RIDE: No overland connection to other featured journeys.

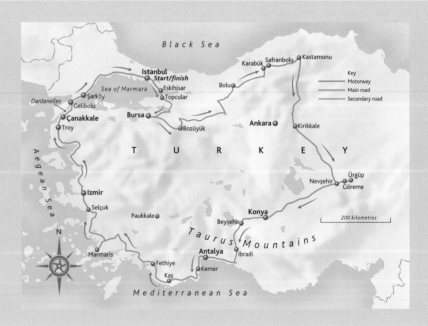

Black Sea

Istanbul
Start/finish

Karabük Safranbolu Kastamonu

Bolu

Eskihisar
Sea of Marmara
Topcular

Şarköy

Dardanelles
Gelibolu

Çanakkale

Troy

Bursa

Bozüyük

Ankara Kırıkkale

Key
Motorway
Main road
Secondary road

T U R K E Y

Ürgüp
Nevşehir
Göreme

Aegean Sea

Izmir

Selçuk

Paukkale

Konya

Beyşehir

200 kilometres

Taurus Mountains

Marmaris

Fethiye

Antalya Ibradi

Kaş Kemer

N

Mediterranean Sea

rock. Watch the sun set on this mysterious moonscape as you sip the local wine, which has been produced in this region for centuries.

It is a fast ride west for 300 km (186 miles) through the agricultural flatlands of central Turkey to Konya, spiritual home of the mystical sect of the Whirling Dervishes. Departing Konya it is a great day's ride across the Taurus Mountains to the Mediterranean Sea. Take the secondary road via Beysehir and Ibradi to Antalya, and you will be rewarded with a fantastic 120 km (75 mile) ride and stunning views. If you want to kick off your boots for a few days, the coastal route is lined with archaeological sites, sandy beaches and innumerable places to stay. If you only visit one Greco-Roman site, it has to be Ephesus, 400 km (249 miles) from Antalya, just outside the town of Selçuk along the Aegean coast. Beautifully preserved, it is easy to spend a day wandering amongst the temples, theatres and baths. It is a huge site and definitely not to be tackled in the heat of the day wearing full leathers!

As you ride north along the Aegean coast, stop to visit the legendary site of Troy, lying just 20 km (12 miles) south of Canakkale. There are regular ferries from Canakkale across the Dardanelles to the Gallipoli peninsula, the scene of terrible fighting during the First World War, and now a national park. From here it is just a few hours' ride back to Istanbul. Barter in the Grand Bazaar, marvel at the opulence of the Ottoman Empire and admire the beautiful skyline on an evening cruise along the Bosphorus.

◁ FAR LEFT *Grand Bazaar, Istanbul.*

◁ LEFT *Swapping saddles.*

▽ *The Taurus Mountains.*

All information was correct at time of going to press. Some of the operators listed below also provide bike hire for riders who don't wish to join a tour.

AFRICA

MOROCCO
Tourist information: www.visitmorocco.org

Wilderness Wheels #61 Hay al-Qods, Ouarzazate 45000, Morocco
Tel: +212 24 88 81 28
Email: infos@wildernesswheels.com
Website: www.wildernesswheels.com

Organizes guided, all-inclusive, off-road tours in Morocco.

KENYA
Tourist information: www.magicalkenya.com

Fredlink Tours & Safari Diani Beach Road, PO Box 85976-80100, Mombasa, Kenya
Tel: +254 403 300 253
Email: fredlink@wanadoo.fr
Websites: www.motorbike-safari.com

Offers off-road tours in Kenya and Tanzania.

NAMIBIA/SOUTH AFRICA
Tourist information: www.namibiatourism.com
www.southafrica.net

Africa Motion Tours PO Box 40685, Windhoek, Namibia
Tel: +264 61 237258
Email: wmotiont@iway.na
Website: www.africamotiontours.com

Specializes in motorcycle and quad bike tours on- and off-road. Also offers a buyback scheme.

Springbok Atlas 179 Albert Road, Woodstock 7925, Cape Town, South Africa
Tel: +27 21 460 4700
Email: andrebjnr@springbokatlas.com
Website: www.springbokatlas.com

Offers tailor-made motorcycle tours and bike hire in Namibia and South Africa.

Karoo Biking CC Loft 4, 5 Howe Street, 7925 Observatory, Cape Town, South Africa
Tel: +27 82 533 6655
Email: info@karoo-biking.de
Website: www.karoo-biking.com

Specializes in on- and off-road tours and BMW motorcycle rentals.

THE AMERICAS

Tourist information: www.canadatourism.ca
www.visitusa.org.uk
www.visitmexico.com
www.visitcostarica.com
www.visit-chile.org
www.argentinaturistica.com

Sturgis Rally www.sturgismotorcyclerally.com

EagleRider 11860 S. La Cienega Blvd, Los Angeles, CA 90250, USA
Tel: +001 310 536 6777
Email: rent@eaglerider.com
Website: www.eaglerider.com

Offers motorcycle tours and rental throughout the USA.

Motorcycle Tour Guide Nova Scotia PO Box 5039, Waverley, NS, BR2 1S2, Canada
Tel: +001 902 861 3521
Email mtrcycletourguid@accesswave.ca
Website: www.motorcycletourguidens.com

A free travel guide available worldwide that includes built-in mapping, detailed routes, photographs and details of touring companies.

MotoDiscovery 22200 Highway 46 West, Spring Branch, Texas 78070 6774, USA
Tel: +830 438 7744
Email: info@motodiscovery.com
Website: www.motodiscovery.com

A US-based company that has been operating for many years in Mexico and Latin America, and has recently expanded into Asia and the Middle East.

Wild Rider Motorcycles Paseo Colón, 30–32 Street, San José, Costa Rica
Tel: +506 258 4604
Email: info@wild-rider.com
Website: www.wild-rider.com

Rental of dual-sport motorcycles (250cc–650cc) guided and self-guided motorcycle tours.

Moto Aventura Torres del Paine 1933, Osorno, Chile
Tel: +56 64 249121
Email: sonia@motoaventura.cl
Website: www.motoaventura.cl

Rental of BMW motorcycles, self-guided organized tours and tailor-made itineraries in Chile, Patagonia, Peru and northern Argentina.

ASIA

SRI LANKA
Tourist information: www.srilankatourism.org

Diana Tours Sha Lanka, 54 Beach Road, Ettukala, Negombo, Sri Lanka
Tel: +94 777 488 746
Email: info@negombo-motorcycle-tours.com
Website: www.negombo-motorcycle-tours.com

Offers guided motorcycle tours and motorcycle hire in Sri Lanka.

INDIA/NEPAL
Tourist information: www.incredibleindia.org

Indian Motorcycle Club
Website: www.60kph.com

Provides information and routes for riding in India.

Himalayan Riders PO Box 13236, Baluwatar, Kathmandu, Nepal
Tel: +997 1442 6695
Email: himalayanriders@gmail.com
Website: www.himalayanmotorcycletours.com

Fixed departure and tailor-made all-inclusive tours in Nepal, Tibet, PRC, Bhutan, China, Sikkim, Darjeeling, Ladakh and Mongolia.

THAILAND
Tourist information: www.tourismthailand.org

The GT Rider
Website: www.gt-rider.com

Travel forum providing information about riding in Thailand.

Siam Enduro 60 Moo 6, T. Khi Lek, A. Mae Tang, Chiang Mai 50150, Thailand
Tel: +66 53 372 189
Email: info@siamenduro.com
Website: www.siamenduro.com

Offers fully guided bike-inclusive Enduro adventure tours in Thailand & Laos.

VIETNAM
Tourist information: www.vietnamtourism.com

Voyage Vietnam/Mototours Asia 1 & 2 Luong Ngoc Quyen St, Hanoi, Vietnam
Tel: +84 4 9 262 616
Email: voyagevietnam@gmail.com
Website: www.moto-tours.org

Offers all-inclusive guided tours in Vietnam and multi-country tours in south Asia, including China, Laos and Cambodia.

CHINA
Tourist information: www.cnto.org

Dragon Bike Tour G/F, No 1, Yin On Street, To Kwa Wan, Kowloon, Hong Kong, China
Tel: +86 852 2147 1010
Email: dragonbiketour@gmail.com
Website: www.dragonbiketour.com

Specializes in motorcycle tours in northwest China, including Silk Road routes and Tibet.

MONGOLIA
Tourist information:
www.mongoliatourism.gov.mn

Off The Map Tours/Bike Mongolia Bayanzurkh District, 13th Microdistrict, Building 4, No 184, Ulaanbaatar, Mongolia
Tel: +976 99 75 43 87
Email: offthemap@magicnet.mn

Website: www.bikemongolia.com

Offers fully supported off-road tours across Mongolia. Branch offices in the UK and Germany.

AUSTRALASIA

AUSTRALIA
Tourist information: www.australia.com

Bikescape 183 Parramatta Road, Young Street, Annandale, NSW 2038, Australia
Tel: +61 2 9569 4111
Email: info@bikescape.com.au
Website: www.bikescape.com.au

Provides all-inclusive motorcycle rentals, self-guided tours and full support services. You can also hire accessories such as helmets and GPS units.

BikeRoundOz 20 Old Admiral Lane, Perth, WA 6112, Australia
Tel: +61 8 9399 2991
Email: info@bikeroundoz.com
Website: www.bikeroundoz.com

Offers motorcycle rentals and self-guided and guided tours from all major cities in Australia.

NEW ZEALAND
Tourist information: www.newzealand.com

Includes a section dedicated to motorcycle tours. There are numerous operators – their contact details can also be found here.

EUROPE

ICELAND
Tourist information: www.visiticeland.com

KTM Adventure Tours Iceland Álfhólsvegur 8, 200 Kópavogur, Iceland
Tel: +354 897 6645
Email: ktm@hive.is
Website: www.ktm-tours.net

Motocross and Enduro rides for experienced and novice dirt bike riders.

NORWAY
Tourist information: www.norway.info

Nordic Bike Adventure Stauslandstunet 26, N-4640 Sogne, Norway
Tel: +47 911 29876
Email: ot@nordicbike.no
Website: www.nordicbike.no

Offers two and three week tours of the west coast fjords and north into the Arctic Circle.

SCOTLAND
Tourist information: www.visitscotland.org

Highland Rider Motorcycle Adventure Holidays Waulkmilton Farm Cottage, Linlithgow EH49 7PU, Scotland
Tel: +44 1506 846 616
Email: peter@highlandrider.com
Website: www.highlandrider.com

Offers guided tours throughout mainland Scotland, the Western Isles, Orkney and Shetland.

IRELAND
Tourist information: www.tourismireland.com

Moto Ireland PO Box 227, Newtownards, BT23 9AU, Northern Ireland
Tel: +44 7709 445 852
Email: john@motoireland.com
Website: www.motoireland.com

Provides a guided tour service including accommodation for those wishing to ride their own bike.

ENGLAND
Tourist information: www.yorkshirevisitor.com

White Rose Motorcycle Tours 3 Springhaven, Hampsthwaite, Harrogate, North Yorkshire HG3 2EG, England
Tel: +44 1423 770 103
Email: info@motorcycletours.co.uk
Website: www.motorcycletours.co.uk

Touring holidays in the UK and Europe. Using your own motorcycle, choose from guided weekend breaks to fully escorted European tours.

H-C Travel Ltd 16 High Street, Overton, Hants, RG25 3HA, England
Tel: +44 1256 770 775
Email: david@hctravel.com
Website: www.hctravel.com

The UK's longest established licensed motorcycle tour operator, offering a variety of tours and motorcycle hire on five continents.

GERMANY
Tourist information: www.germany-tourism.de

The Nürburgring
Website: www.nuerburgring.de

Official website of the Nürburgring.

FRANCE
Tourist information: www.franceguide.com

Upright Tours 6 Route de la Boulzane,11140 Puilaurens, France
Tel : +33 468 207 334
Email: info@uprighttours.co.uk
Website: www.uprighttours.co.uk

Pyrenees specialists, offering guided and self-guided tours and bike hire.

SPAIN
Tourist information: www.spain.info

Iberian Moto Tours Calle Chapineria 6B, Pol. Ind. Ventorro del Cano, 28925 Alcorcón, Madrid, Spain
Tel: +34 91 591 3482
Email: info@imtbike.com
Website: www.imtbike.com

Offers rentals in seven different locations in Spain. They also offer fully guided and self-guided tours in Spain, Portugal and Morocco.

THE ALPS
Tourist information: www.austria.info
www.myswitzerland.com

Grossglockner Pass
Website: www.grossglockner.com

The official website of the most famous motorcycle pass in the Alps.

Edelweiss Bike Travel Reise GmbH. Sportplatzweg 14, 6414 Mieming, Austria
Tel: +43 5264 5690
Email: worldtours@edelweissbike.com
Website: www.edelweissbike.com

Worldwide, fully supported guided motorcycle tours, including numerous European destinations.

ITALY
Tourist information: www.suedtirol.info
www.trentino.to

Club Mototurismo Via Solteri n. 78, 38100 Trento, Italy
Tel: +39 0461 880 430
Email: info@trentnoinmoto.com
Website: www.trentinoinmoto.com

Official motorcycle club for the Trentino Area. They produce a booklet/map for motorcyclists.

SLOVENIA
Tourist information: www.slovenia.info

Adriatic Moto Tours Ovcakova 12,1211 Ljubljana–Smartno, Slovenia
Tel: +11 386 41 332 418
Email: info@adriaticmototours.com
Website: www.adriaticmototours.com

Organizes fully supported guided tours and self-guided tours around Slovenia, Croatia's Adriatic coast, Montenegro, Czech Republic and Hungary.

TURKEY
Tourist information: www.tourismturkey.org

Kazoom Moto Adventures Abidei Hurriyet Cad 224/1, Sisli, Istanbul 34381, Turkey
Tel: +90 212 233 0075
Email: kazoom@kazoom-moto-adventures.com
Website www.kazoom-moto-adventures.com

Fully guided or self-guided tours of Turkey and neighbouring countries including Syria, Jordan, Iran and Black Sea countries.

PICTURE CREDITS